THE
CEREAL KILLER
CHRONICLES
—— OF ——
BATTLE CREEK

THE
CEREAL KILLER
CHRONICLES
OF
BATTLE CREEK

Jenn Carpenter

THE
History
PRESS

Published by The History Press
Charleston, SC
www.historypress.com

Front cover image courtesy of Erica Cooper, 2020.

First published 2021

Manufactured in the United States

ISBN 9781467149495

Library of Congress Control Number: 2021937168

For my sons, Austin and Ethan. May you always be bold enough to be the Froot Loop in a bowl of Cheerios, and may you always have the courage to follow your dreams—no matter how outlandish they may seem.

CONTENTS

Preface   9
Acknowledgements   11
Introduction   13

The Mad Doctor   19
The San   29
Things We Lost in the Fire   39
The Cereal King   51
The Wildflower   60
The Hitman   71
Three Little Birds   80
The Monster   93

Conclusion   111
Bibliography   119
About the Author   125

PREFACE

Humans are creatures of habit. We all have our traditions and routines, our idiosyncrasies that others may view as odd, but that make us who we are. One strange custom of mine is that I have to have a bowl of cereal every night before bed. Ever since I was young, the last thing I do before turning in each night is pour a bowl of Froot Loops or some other sugary confection, drown it with milk and crunch away to my heart's content. If, for some reason, I fall asleep before my requisite bowl of cereal, I will inevitably wake up in the middle of the night craving a little snap, crackle, pop—2:00 a.m., 4:00 a.m., it doesn't matter. I will find my way through the dark to the kitchen, make a bowl of cereal (or two) and often turn on the TV while I eat. As a true crime aficionado, my TV is almost always tuned to one of those channels that airs true crime documentaries 24/7. It was on one such night, while I was eating cereal and watching murder shows, that *The Cereal Killer Chronicles* was born.

As the host of a podcast that focuses on true crime and weird history in Michigan, I'm always looking for stories to cover. On this particular night, as I was munching away on my Froot Loops during the wee hours, I had a thought: cereal was invented in Michigan. (This wouldn't turn out to be exactly true, but this is how it all began, so just bear with me.) The Kelloggs were from Michigan, I remembered. They created cereal while working on recipes for patients at their sanitarium. The Kelloggs ran a sanitarium. Wait—*the* Kelloggs, the rulers of the cereal world, ran a sanitarium in Michigan. I was instantly upset with myself that I was a full year and a half into my podcast before it dawned on me that the Kelloggs might make an interesting topic of conversation. With my thoughts in overdrive and the possibility of sleep out the window, I fired up my laptop and jumped willingly down the rabbit hole of Kellogg history. It's fitting that my research began with *The Road to Wellville*, a quirky, off-beat movie based on the novel by the same name, because the next several weeks were truly a journey.

During my fact-finding mission, I kept coming across stories that were not directly connected to the Kellogg family, per se, but their legacy. Some of the employees at their cereal factory and students of their university were involved in unspeakable crimes—some as victims and others as cold-blooded killers.

In this book, you'll learn about the rise of the Kelloggs, from their days as religious fanatics to their breakfast food empire, and all of the death and darkness in between. You'll also learn about their enduring legacy in Battle Creek, from the ghosts they left behind to the curse that appears to haunt those who work and learn in Kellogg-built institutions.

ACKNOWLEDGEMENTS

History must be preserved in order for others to write about it, so I would like to extend the humblest of thank yous to those who work so hard to conserve our past by saving and digitizing documents, newspapers and photographs for future generations to reference. I would also like to thank those who put in hundreds upon hundreds of hours of research to write comprehensive works on the subjects covered in this book. The Willard Library in Battle Creek and the work of Dr. Howard J. Markel were especially important to this project. To my dear friend and colleague Erica Cooper of Erica Jo Photography, who provided many of the breathtaking images in this publication, thank you! There is no one I'd rather explore a cemetery with. To my husband, Dax, and our boys for taking care of the dogs and the house while I spent months living in an alternative universe ruled by cereal and killers, thank you, and I love you. Thanks also to all of my friends and family members who took time out of their busy schedules to proofread the book and provide feedback. Lastly, I must thank the Kelloggs themselves, not only for creating the world's most versatile meal, but also for being so delightfully odd and awful that they still inspire the creators of today.

INTRODUCTION

The publisher of this work offers no apology for presenting it to the reading public, since the wide prevalence of the evils which it exposes is sufficient warrant for its publication.
—Dr. J.H. Kellogg, 1877

Where the Battle Creek and Kalamazoo Rivers converge, you'll find Cereal City USA, an urban metropolis with a strange and fascinating history. Named after a bloody battle between Natives and nineteenth-century land surveyors, Battle Creek was the birthplace of Seventh-day Adventists (SDA) and an integral part of the Underground Railroad. It was also home to the Kelloggs, a family of eccentric inventors and entrepreneurs who would go on to rule the world of breakfast foods. But before their worldwide fame came the sanitarium—and the questionable deaths and the fires. And after their downfall came the complicated legacy that would continue to result in tragedy for decades to come. Cereal is Battle Creek's lifeblood, but it has also been the root cause of bloodshed in the city many times over.

With a modern-day population of just over fifty thousand, Battle Creek is classified as a small city, but it was once home to giants. Like most Michigan cities, its first settlers were Natives. Around 1774, the Potawatomi and Ottawa tribes formed a village where two wild rivers met. They lived in relative peace for years. But in 1817, construction began on a navigable water route from New York and the Atlantic Ocean to the Great Lakes. As

Downtown Battle Creek. *Courtesy of Erica Cooper, 2020.*

the Erie Canal neared completion, the U.S. government began surveying the new land that would soon be accessible to the overpopulated puritanical colonies on the East Coast. In anticipation of what would soon become known as "Michigan Fever," land was to be charted, sectioned off and sold to hopeful pioneers. Sure, they were selling land that was already home to Native tribes, but there was another plan in the works to remedy that.

By 1825, surveying of the area that was soon to be known as Battle Creek was well underway. Led by Colonel John Mullett, surveyors set up camp near what is now the Battle Creek River. Their presence disrupted the way of life the local Native tribes were accustomed to. As life got noisier and busier, the wildlife that had once been in such abundance in the area grew scarce. The woods were over-hunted, the rivers were over-fished, and soon, the tribes began struggling to find food. Per a treaty with the government, the Army was supposed to provide food and supplies to the tribe, but their deliveries were often late, resulting in dangerous food shortages.

On March 14, 1825, two members of the Potawatomi tribe approached the surveyors' camp to ask for flour and other provisions. The surveyors refused to help them, and after a war of words, the altercation turned physical. In some retellings of the tale, one of the tribesmen was shot but not killed. In other versions, a rifle was pulled to scare the men off

Downtown Battle Creek, circa the 1800s. *Courtesy of the Willard Library Historical Collection.*

but not fired. According to the surveyors, no guns were involved, but one of the Potawatomi men was shoved to the ground. Later that night, as the surveyors were joking about the dust-up, Colonel Mullett asked what they should call the "dangerous" stream. One of his men joked, "Call it Battle Creek." Colonel Mullett wrote the name down, and it stuck. While many historians refer to the skirmish that led to the naming of a city as a "bloody battle," the only thing wounded was a man's pride.

The Potawatomi were forced from their land following the Indian Removal Act of 1830, and in 1831, English settlers moved in. Quaker Sands

McCamly is widely credited with founding the first village at Battle Creek, and by the 1840s, the community was thriving as a center for grain, flour, and sawmills.

In 1839, Erastus Hussey and his wife, Sarah, moved from New York to Battle Creek, where they opened a general store. The Husseys were outspoken abolitionists and soon began hiding those who escaped slavery in their home. Erastus became a politician and held seats in both the Michigan House of Representatives and the Michigan Senate. He was a founding member of the Republican Party and the publisher of the abolitionist newspaper *Michigan Liberty Press*. Before long, the Hussey abode became a major stop on the Underground Railroad, and Erastus and Sarah, known as "station masters," helped over one thousand enslaved people escape to freedom. Rather than flee to Canada, which was the original plan, many of those freed people chose to settle in Battle Creek. They built homes, businesses and churches and were welcomed into the community. As a result, Battle Creek gained a reputation as a safe haven for those fleeing slavery and abolitionists alike. This is why, after first visiting the city in 1856, famed abolitionist, women's rights activist and former enslaved American Sojourner Truth decided to make Battle Creek her home.

Erastus Hussey and Sojourner Truth are featured in the *Memorial to the Underground Railroad* sculpture at Kellogg House Park. *Courtesy of Erica Cooper, 2020.*

Formerly Isabella Bomfree, Truth was born into slavery in 1797 in New York. At the age of nine, she was sold, along with a flock of sheep, for one hundred dollars to a man who tortured and beat her daily. She was bought and sold several more times over the next few years. During this time, she was raped and beaten regularly. She was then purchased by John Dumont of West Park, New York, when she was just thirteen years old. Dumont was a cruel man who raped and abused Truth even after she married an enslaved man by the name of Thomas. Truth birthed five children between 1815 and 1826, fathered by both her husband and her owner.

When she finally escaped her sadistic owner in 1826, Sojourner was only able to take her youngest child, infant Sophia, with her. She found safety in the home of abolitionists Isaac and Maria Van Wagenen, who helped her sue the Alabama slave owner who had illegally purchased her five-year-old son. Sojourner eventually got her son back and became the first Black woman to win in court against a white man.

Even as a free woman, Sojourner's life was not an easy one. Unable to read or write, she moved around the country and took housekeeping jobs wherever she could find them. She was once accused of murdering her boss but was later acquitted. Her son Peter was lost at sea while working on a whaling ship. She was a lost soul. But in 1843, she was found. She became devoutly religious and changed her name to Sojourner Truth, saying that the spirit of God had called on her to preach the truth. She began traveling the country, attending spiritual retreats and gatherings and giving motivational speeches.

On September 3, 1857, Truth sold all of her earthly possessions and moved to Battle Creek. Not only was it a battleground for abolitionists, it was also where her three daughters had settled with their families, and it was a home base for her church. There, she continued her work as an abolitionist and activist and became a local legend.

As slavery ended and the Underground Railroad became obsolete, a new religion was invading the city between two rivers—the Seventh-day Adventists. With them came the family who would change the face of Battle Creek forever.

THE MAD DOCTOR

When the man who would turn the medical community on its head was first born, he was anything but the picture of health. As a child, he was so sickly that his parents feared he wouldn't live to adulthood. In an effort to understand his own body, the boy began studying medicine at a young age. Surrounded by religious fanatics with odd ideas about healthcare, his interest soon became an obsession. In his quest to live to the age of one hundred, the mad doctor's treatments were anything but standard. Known as a charismatic genius, sickly people from around the world flocked to his controversial institution in Battle Creek for care. But instead of finding wellness, many of them met horrific fates instead.

John Harvey Kellogg was born on February 26, 1852, to John and Ann Kellogg, one of seventeen children. The family lived in Tyrone Township, a small community in Michigan's Livingston County. They were a family of mixed parentage. The five eldest children were born to John Sr. and his first wife, Mary Ann, who died when her children were still young. John Sr. remarried, and with his new wife, he had twelve more children. John Harvey was the eldest son of the second set of Kellogg children, right in the middle overall.

His parents were devoutly religious and were instrumental in bringing the Seventh-day Adventist movement to life. Seventh-day Adventists are a branch of Protestant Christians that grew out of the Millerite movement in the mid-1800s. Millerites were followers of Baptist preacher William Miller, who proclaimed Jesus would return to Earth on October 22, 1844.

When that didn't happen, the date of the supposed rapture became known as the "Great Disappointment." Most of Miller's followers abandoned him. They were, after all, greatly disappointed. But a small group, including self-proclaimed prophet Ellen White, had a different interpretation of Miller's prophecy. According to the diehard Millerites, their leader had the date right, but his idea of what was supposed to happen was wrong. October 22, 1844 wasn't Judgment Day after all, it was Prejudgment Day. The end was still coming.

John and Ann Kellogg were banking on the whole rapture idea and, therefore, didn't bother to do very basic things like educate their children. What's the point if the end of the world is nigh? Following the Great Disappointment, they sought out the very small faction of Millerites who still believed the Second Coming was upon them. Faced with the reality of having to homeschool seventeen children, the Kelloggs needed to believe the world was ending.

So, plan B became bringing these doomsday fanatics to Michigan. John and Ann Kellogg pledged a substantial sum of money to bring Ellen White and her husband, James, to Battle Creek, where they would run their religious propaganda printing company and their start-up ministry. The Whites arrived in Battle Creek in 1854, and the Kelloggs followed them in 1856.

The Seventh-day Adventist Church was officially founded on May 21, 1863, in Battle Creek, where its headquarters would remain for decades. While a large part of the ministry was focused on the second coming of Christ, the church also put an emphasis on healthy living. It believed that the human body represented God's temple, and therefore, it should not be abused. In fact, Mother White, as she came to be known, is considered a leading figure in American vegetarian history.

John Harvey Kellogg did not have an easy childhood. He was small and sickly, often referred to as the runt of the litter. Even as an adult, he only grew to be five foot, four inches tall. As a boy, he had tuberculosis, which left him with a nonfunctioning lung. He was plagued with digestive issues, including colitis. He was so unwell that his parents often worried he wouldn't live a long life. Because of this, John Sr. distanced himself from John Harvey, but Ann coddled him.

John Harvey only had about two years of official schooling as a child. He attended school in Battle Creek from ages nine to eleven before leaving to help in his father's broom factory. During his downtime between long hours at the factory sorting brooms, John Harvey taught himself to read. Turns out,

Ellen White, circa 1864. *Courtesy of the Ellen G. White estate.*

he was whip-smart, and he quickly became his mother's favorite of all her children. That's a big deal when you're one of seventeen.

When he was twelve, John Harvey began working for Mother White at her printing business. He started out as an errand boy but quickly rose to proofreading and editing. To do his work, he had to read and reread the materials the Whites were publishing, so he quickly became an expert on Mother White's theories and beliefs regarding health and began following them strictly.

John Harvey wanted to be a teacher, and in 1868, at the age of sixteen, he began teaching at a school in Hastings, a small town about twenty-five miles north of Battle Creek.

John Harvey Kellogg in 1875. *Courtesy of the Willard Library Historical Collection.*

He oversaw the education of forty students while still finishing his own studies. When he was twenty, John enrolled in a teacher's training course at Michigan State Normal School in Ypsilanti, now known as Eastern Michigan University. He graduated in 1872, but before he could begin his career as a teacher, his parents and the Whites, who had become like his pseudo-parents, needed something else from him.

The Whites had decided to open a wellness institute, and rather than bring in doctors from the outside world who might have their own medical opinions, the Whites wanted some of their own to become doctors. So, John Harvey, along with his older brother Merritt and two of the Whites' sons, traveled to New Jersey for a six-month medical course at Russell Trall's Hygieo-Therapeutic College, paid for by the Whites. The college specialized in hydropathy, or "the water cure." The water cure is a broad term for a wide range of treatments for pain and illness using water. The school also focused on dietary therapies, hygiene, exercise, and abandoning modern medicine in favor of alternative treatments.

John Harvey excelled in the program and went on to attend medical school at the University of Michigan and New York University, all on Mother White's dime. He obtained his medical degree in 1875, and on October 1, 1876, at the age of twenty-four, Dr. John Harvey Kellogg became the director of the Whites' Western Health Reform Institute. He began making changes right away, starting with the name. He wanted the institute to be a place like no other, which meant it had to have a name like no other. So, Dr.

Kellogg quite literally made up his own word: *sanitarium*, which is derived from the word *sanatorium*. In Dr. Kellogg's opinion, *sanatorium* had negative connotations attached to it. Sanatoriums were hospitals for invalids and the chronically ill. Basically, people went there to die.

The doctor's sanitarium, on the other hand, was a place for people to recover and to learn how to stay well. Some might have suggested just choosing a different word altogether, but Dr. Kellogg did a lot of things that didn't make sense to other people—as we'll come to find out. So, he renamed the facility the Battle Creek Sanitarium. "The San," as it became known, was a wild place that made headlines all over the globe. It was frequented by celebrities, praised and condemned for its practices, and became a vacation destination for the world's elite. But running the infamous sanitarium wasn't even the most interesting thing about the mad doctor. There was so much more.

For instance, Dr. Kellogg was a married man with forty-two children, but he died a virgin. Until the 1970s, Seventh-day Adventists believed in celibacy outside of procreation, which meant that once you were married, you could have sex to procreate, but that was it—and you certainly weren't supposed to enjoy it. Dr. Kellogg took this belief to the extreme and remained celibate his entire life, even after he was married. There were rumors that a nasty bout of mumps as a child left him impotent, but those were never confirmed. "Sex is the sewer drain of a healthy body," he would say. Masturbation was also an illicit act—an even bigger no-no than sex, actually. According to Dr. Kellogg, "Masturbation is the silent killer of the night." He believed it caused poor digestion, memory loss, impaired vision, heart disease, epilepsy, insanity and more. To keep boys from committing such sinful deeds, he suggested their parents tie their hands, bandage "the appendage," put a cage around it and, if none of that worked, circumcision without anesthetic. His hope was that the searing pain would have a permanent effect on the brain, curing the patient of their unholy desires. His treatment plan for girls was worse. He favored applying pure carbolic acid to the clitoris to burn and permanently damage it. And in more extreme cases, he recommended surgical removal of the clitoris, also known as a female circumcision.

Though he remained chaste throughout his life, Dr. Kellogg did get married. On February 22, 1879, just a few days before his twenty-seventh birthday, he married twenty-five-year-old Ella Ervilla Eaton of New York, who he met when she was a patient at the sanitarium. The couple kept separate bedrooms for their entire forty-year marriage, which was easy to do because their house had over twenty bedrooms. While that sounds over the

Christmas Eve in the Kellogg home, circa 1906. *Courtesy of the Michigan Bentley Historical Library.*

top, it was necessary; over the years, the Kelloggs fostered forty-two children, permanently adopting eight of them.

Another odd fact about Dr. Kellogg was that he always dressed in white from head to toe—white suit jacket and pants, white shirt, white tie, white socks, white shoes, white hat when the occasion called for it and, often, a white cockatoo perched on his shoulder. One of the cornerstones of the Battle Creek Sanitarium was teaching personal hygiene techniques. Granted, in the 1800s, especially, hygiene was a legitimate concern. But like most things, Dr. Kellogg took it to the extreme. He was worried that if he dressed in dark clothing, he would get dirt and germs on him without knowing it, and that was unacceptable. If he was dressed in all white, any stains would show, and he could (and would) go change immediately. There was no medical or scientific reason for the bird, though; he just loved animals.

Dr. Kellogg was very particular about his animals. As a result, he's the reason there are black squirrels in Mid-Michigan. The bushy-tailed rodents were actually native to Michigan once upon a time, but squirrel hunters decimated their population because they were easier to spot than their brown and gray counterparts. Dr. Kellogg grew up in an area where black squirrels were prevalent, and he missed seeing them around. So he had hundreds

Dr. Kellogg and his pet cockatoo. *Courtesy of the Library of Congress.*

of them shipped to the sanitarium in 1915 and let them loose. Through his family's work with scientists and universities, a small number of black squirrels wound up at Michigan State University in East Lansing, where they were released into the wild.

Another random fact about Dr. Kellogg: he was so fanatical about his digestive health that he reportedly gave himself five enemas a day. Enemas were a big part of the treatment program at the Battle Creek Sanitarium, as they were said to be vital to maintaining a healthy colon. In this instance, at least, the doctor practiced what he preached.

Not everything about the good doctor was good, however. In 1906, he founded the Race Betterment Foundation as his contribution to the eugenics movement. Eugenics was a calculated, misguided attempt to improve the genetic composition of the human race by scientifically weeding out "undesirable traits" through selective breeding. It involved identifying and classifying "degenerate" and "unfit" individuals based on race, sexuality, mental fitness, financial stability, promiscuity, and disability—then eradicating them. Dr. Kellogg didn't want what he considered "imperfections" dirtying his immaculate gene pool.

He didn't consider himself a racist, however. Of his forty-two foster children, many of them were people of color. He built a community swimming pool for the neighborhood children and all were welcome, which was rare at the turn of the century. People of color could swim in Dr. Kellogg's actual pool—just not his gene pool. He prohibited segregation at the sanitarium as well. He kept men and women separated but did not allow separation based on skin color. When his friend and neighbor Sojourner Truth needed a skin graft, he gave her some of his own skin. When she died, she had a thick band of white flesh on one of her arms, courtesy of Dr. Kellogg. He was compassionate, generous, and loving toward people of color, but he never considered them his equals, and he had no idea how racist that actually made him. He didn't dislike people of color; he just didn't want them mixing with his "superior" white race. In 1902, he wrote, "The intellectual inferiority of the negro male to the European male is universally acknowledged," proving only that he surrounded himself with people who were just as racist as he was.

It wasn't only race that drove the eugenics and race betterment movement, however. Through his role on the Michigan Board of Health, Dr. Kellogg promoted a bill that was passed by the legislature in 1913: Public Act 34, an act to authorize the sterilization of "mentally defective" persons so that they could not reproduce and spread their "unpure" genes. Close to four thousand Michiganders were involuntarily sterilized under this law that was touted by Dr. Kellogg, including moral degenerates, sexual deviants, epileptics, and the insane. The sterilization act wasn't repealed until 1974.

Dr. John Harvey Kellogg was a philanthropic racist, a celibate father, a sexist husband and a lover of enemas and black squirrels. He was offensive and off-putting, but oddly charismatic. He was a giant personality inside a tiny body. He was the physical embodiment of a "mad scientist," but he was also an inventor. Here are some of the things he is credited with inventing, although a few of these have been disputed over the years as others filed patents around the same time he did: peanut butter, granola, electric blankets, loofahs, soy milk, and the big one—cereal. While Dr. Kellogg is widely credited with creating the world's first flaked cereal, just how his most glorious creation came to be remains up for debate.

The doctor was a health guru. He ran a world-renowned wellness resort, and he took his job very seriously. He knew what he wanted his patients to eat, and he was always looking for new and innovative ways to serve it to them. The bulk of the menu at the sanitarium was made up of whole grains, which can be tricky to serve without a lot of additives. Dr. Kellogg would experiment with different grains by creating a paste-like dough that he would then try to turn into food that was at least easily digestible if not tasty—not too mushy, but not so hard that people broke their teeth while chewing, which happened on occasion in the doctor's kitchen.

Creating nutritious, ready-to-eat, affordable breakfast food had been an idea of Dr. Kellogg's since his college days, when he was always short on money and time. It became even more important to him once he became responsible for the nutrition of the thousands of patients at the sanitarium. According to the doctor, the idea of flaked cereal came to him in a dream, and he tasked his wife, Ella, and his little brother Will with helping him make that dream a reality. But no matter what they tried, it didn't work. They couldn't turn their wheat, oat, and corn mush into the airy, flaky morsels Dr. Kellogg had envisioned.

The precise details of how Dr. Kellogg and his crew were finally successful in making cereal flakes are unclear, as the key players all told different versions of the story. But essentially, a batch of wheat dough that had been allowed to go stale was run through a set of rollers and came out in the thin flakes the doctor had been dreaming of. Letting the dough turn stale before rolling it was what finally made the difference. The Kelloggs then toasted the flakes and served them to their patients, who ate them up—literally. On May 31, 1895, a patent was filed by Dr.

Kellogg for "flaked cereals and process of preparing same." The patent was granted on April 14, 1896. This patented flaking process was later applied to corn mush, which resulted, of course, in Kellogg's Corn Flakes, the first breakfast cereal to be devoured by the masses.

The invention of corn flakes changed the fate and legacy of the Kelloggs. It resulted in a bitter feud that tore the family apart and lasted to the grave. It changed the face of a city and the idea of what constituted a healthy American breakfast. It also led to theft, lawsuits, sabotage, and even death. But before the cereal empire, there was the San.

THE SAN

Ask one hundred people what Dr. Kellogg's greatest achievement was, and ninety-nine of them will tell you it was the invention of cereal. But they'd all be wrong, because Dr. Kellogg neither invented cereal nor was it the thing he was most proud of. His crowning achievement—his life's work—was the Battle Creek Sanitarium, also known as "The San."

Sanitarium, to paraphrase Inigo Montoya: I do not think it means what you think it means. I know that I didn't have a clue what a sanitarium was or, rather, what Dr. Kellogg meant for it to be, before I started this project. I watch a lot of paranormal shows, and sanitariums, asylums, institutions—they're all one and the same. They're awful places where people who were unwell in one way or another were locked away and subjected to unspeakable torture and neglect. But Dr. Kellogg's sanitarium wasn't a house of horrors. On the surface, at least, it was a state-of-the-art wellness center frequented by the elites of the late nineteenth and early twentieth centuries. It didn't start out that way, though.

The Western Health Reform Institute of Battle Creek was established by Ellen White and her Seventh-day Adventist Church on September 5, 1867, when Dr. Kellogg was still just a fifteen-year-old boy. It was built on a principle Mother White had adopted following one of her many visions, which historians today believe were more likely epileptic seizures than prophecies from God. Mother White told her followers that God had come to her and emphasized the importance of a life in harmony with dietary and lifestyle principles designed to help one stay well and prevent disease. She issued a health reform doctrine focused on hygiene, diet, and chastity, and this was the basis for the institute.

The first building was a two-story wooden structure attached to an old, rundown house, with the ability to treat sixteen patients per month. It had no electricity or modern plumbing; it was sparsely furnished and lit with oil lamps. It was dark, moldy, smelly and just all around unpleasant—kind of exactly what you'd expect a sanitarium from the 1800s might be. But people weren't "committed" to Mother White's institute or held there against their will. Guests, primarily followers of the Seventh-day Adventist faith, went to the institute voluntarily, hoping to benefit from the healing powers of water. They never returned, however. The institute didn't have a single repeat customer, which speaks volumes about the condition of the place.

There were three treatment rooms at the facility, where patients were treated to thrice-daily baths, water sprays, and wet pad treatments. The water used for all of this was pumped in from the Kalamazoo River, courtesy of a windmill. So, when there was no wind or a drought left the river levels low, the institute had to conserve the water and had guests reuse each other's bathwater.

Suffice it to say, things were not going well for the Whites at their institute, and around the time Dr. Kellogg obtained his medical degree from New York University, the Whites asked the doctor's father, John Sr., to step in and take over management of their struggling health and wellness facility. He agreed to help, but only if he could make his son, the new doctor, the center's director.

The Whites had always planned for Dr. Kellogg to treat patients at the institute—that's why they paid his way through medical school. But they didn't necessarily intend for him to run it. They had two sons of their own who were training to be doctors, and they likely intended to keep the institute in the family. But at the rate things were going, there wouldn't be anything left for them to leave to their children if something didn't change. So the Whites agreed. But Dr. Kellogg had some stipulations of his own. He would only take over the facility if the Whites would grant him free rein to run things with no interference from the church. They begrudgingly obliged.

On October 1, 1876, a twenty-four-year-old Dr. Kellogg, fresh out of medical school, took the helm of the institute for what was originally a one-year trial period. He began making changes immediately. The first thing he changed was the facility's name; he changed it from the Western Health Reform Institute of Battle Creek to the Battle Creek Sanitarium. He didn't like the word *reform*. People don't like to be "reformed." And *sanatorium* wasn't right either, because he wasn't just going to be taking patients in to let them languish in their final days. His facility would be the first of its kind, so it needed a name all its own.

The day Dr. Kellogg took over, there were twenty patients at the institute. Within a few years, he'd expanded from a two-story converted home to a sprawling city within a city that treated seven to ten thousand patients a year. By comparison, when the Whites were running things, they saw a total of two thousand patients over the course of ten years. The sanitarium's main building was a five-story monstrosity with wrap-around verandas on every level. The structure had a brick exterior but was made of wood. The furnaces, air filtration systems and plumbing were all top-of-the-line. There was a one-thousand-seat auditorium for lectures and a hydrotherapy center with over fifty types of baths.

The San was a hit. People from all over traveled to Battle Creek to be treated by the magnetic Dr. Kellogg, including the Lincolns, the Rockefellers, the Fords, Thomas Edison, and even Amelia Earheart, who would visit the San to refresh and recharge before her flights. But what were patients at the San being treated for, exactly? The answer is autointoxication, primarily, a disease that didn't actually exist at all. It was *the* ailment of the turn of the century and was diagnosed in patients who were presenting with symptoms including fatigue, depression, anxiety, digestive issues, chronic headaches, and epilepsy, among others. The belief was that toxins in the gut, usually

MAIN BUILDING, DEDICATED 1878, WITH FIRST ADDITION MADE IN 1884.

The original Battle Creek Sanitarium. *Courtesy of the Willard Library Historical Collection.*

caused by poor eating habits, were poisoning the body, resulting in a wide range of awful maladies. In reality, many of the ailments attributed to autointoxication were very real medical conditions that needed to be treated individually, not as one big catch-all disease.

But even though autointoxication wasn't real, and even though a lot of his beliefs were either completely bonkers or downright evil, some of Dr. Kellogg's holistic treatments and ideas weren't totally off base. He believed in what he called biologic living, which combined his vast scientific knowledge with his Seventh-day Adventist beliefs. Biologic living involved regular vigorous exercise, massage therapy, a focus on spirituality, an abundance of fresh air, avoiding stressors, a lot of sleep, and a lot of water. The big no-nos for those leading the biologic living lifestyle were meat, sugar, caffeine, drugs (both legal and illegal), tobacco, alcohol, sex, and masturbation, which Dr. Kellogg referred to as "self-pollution." A person who practiced biologic living properly could expect to have four to five bowel movements a day. At the San, keeping track of one's bowel movements was a requirement.

To help patients transition from autointoxication to biologic living, Dr. Kellogg had a plethora of tricks up his perfectly white sleeve. His favorite? Enemas. Dr. Kellogg invented enema machines that could pump fifteen quarts of water into the colon in under a minute. After the water enema came a yogurt enema. In addition to rectal yogurt, patients were expected to eat a pint of yogurt every day. While probiotics are still used today to treat digestive issues, Dr. Kellogg's use of them was excessive. Those who opted not to have various liquids rectally administered had other options. Dr. Kellogg had a number of odd contraptions that violently bounced, vibrated, tilted, and twisted patients to free up their bowels.

Some of the treatments offered by the mad doctor and his staff of over one thousand employees were pretty standard, and what you would expect to find at a health and wellness resort even today. There were outdoor sports, physical training classes, spa treatments, health lectures, massages, cooking demonstrations, and daily consultations with physicians and dieticians. And then there were the not-so-standard services, like the enemas—both yogurt and non. Electric light baths, which Dr. Kellogg invented to treat depression and insomnia, were wooden cabinets lined with lightbulbs that the patient would either lay or stand in for an allotted amount of time. This artificial light was said to improve one's mood, especially during the dreary Michigan winters. Electrotherapy, also known as electro-shock therapy, was used primarily to treat obesity. With a contraption he pieced together from parts of an old telephone, the doctor would administer mild doses of electrical

Sanitarium patients enjoying the fresh air. *Courtesy of the Michigan Bentley Historical Library.*

currents directly to his patients' skin in an attempt to burn fat cells. And then there were the baths. There were hot baths, cold baths, electric baths, foot baths, continuous baths that could last for days at a time, mud baths, clay baths, and salt baths. Between the baths and the enemas, patients were almost always being put into various liquids or having various liquids put into them.

Aside from the strange contraptions—some of which bordered on torture devices—there was a nutritional component to treatment at the San. Dr. Kellogg personally crafted a mostly vegan and entirely vegetarian menu of easily digestible foods for his patients. To do this, he had to create many of the foods himself, as he was light-years ahead of his time when it came to health foods. And it wasn't just about what his patients ate—it was about how they ate. In the dining hall at the San, there was a big black-and-white sign that read, "Fletcherize." Fletcherizing was the practice of chewing each bite of food at least forty times before swallowing; that way, it was already partially digested before it hit the digestive track. There was even a song patients were required to sing in the dining hall before every meal about the importance of chewing.

When the water cures, weird exercises, and healthy foods didn't effectively cure patients at the San, Dr. Kellogg used surgery as a last resort, often removing part of the intestine to get the digestive track back in working order. He was said to have performed over twenty-two thousand

Sanitarium patients engaging in outdoor exercise. *Courtesy of the Michigan Bentley Historical Library.*

of these surgeries during his time at the San. While many of his methods and beliefs were questionable, there was no doubt that the doctor was passionate about his job. Despite the fact that he was busy from sunup to sundown and beyond, he personally treated 75 percent of the patients who matriculated through the San—over 130,000 in total. And he didn't even take a salary. He made his money through the sales of his health foods, books, and surgical procedures. He cared deeply about his patients, and he took it to heart when they died, which, unfortunately, happened a lot. It happened so often, in fact, this his younger brother Will was known as the facility's unofficial undertaker.

One death at the San was that of Wayne Wheeler, a prominent attorney and leader of the Anti-Saloon League. Wheeler was so passionate about Prohibition that he led the charge to add poison to industrial alcohol to deter people from drinking it. He believed that the government was under no obligation to protect the lives of its citizens if they chose to break the law and consume industrial alcohol, and that doing so was tantamount

THE SANITARIUM – BATTLE CREEK, MICH. 244.

The Battle Creek Sanitarium, circa 1905. *Courtesy of the Willard Library Historical Collection.*

to choosing suicide. Roughly ten thousand Americans died as a result of drinking government-poisoned alcohol, and Wayne Wheeler was held partially responsible. He retired to escape the public scrutiny, but peace was not to be his. While vacationing at his summer home in Little Point Sable, Michigan, his wife burned to death in a kitchen fire. Her father, who was vacationing with them, had a heart attack and died trying to save his daughter. A distraught Wheeler checked himself into the San following the tragedy. He was said to be recuperating nicely, his condition improving, when one afternoon, he asked a nurse to hand him a book. He sat up halfway in bed to reach for it, and as he did, his heart gave out, and he died suddenly at the age of fifty-seven.

Wayne Wheeler's death was similar to that of prominent Miami physician Dr. William Gramling. The fifty-five-year-old was being treated at the San for a chronic illness and had just written his brother a letter saying he felt better. But before he could send the letter out, he was dead—also of a sudden heart attack. Wealthy glass manufacturer William Porter of Fort Smith, Arkansas, was being treated at the San for a nervous breakdown. He began threatening suicide and was assigned a special nurse to watch over him. He escaped from his nurse and was missing for eight days before a hunter found his remains in the woods near the San. John Hays, a sixty-six-year-old businessman from

Union City, Pennsylvania, was a patient at the San when he was found shot to death in his room. The coroner ruled his death an apparent suicide.

And then there was the "spinach incident." Three patients died of botulism at Blodgett Hospital in Grand Rapids, Michigan, in a very short period, prompting an investigation. That investigation led to tainted spinach that all three victims were believed to have eaten. The spinach was traced back to a canning company in California. As it turned out, the spinach was part of a large order that was shipped to several locations, so officials then had to track it all down. One of the places the spinach was sent to was the San. When questioned, management admitted to officials that several otherwise healthy employees had recently died but that if it was from tainted spinach, they didn't get it at the San, as they were known to eat outside of the establishment. To confuse matters further, the San hastily put out a statement saying that no one at the facility had died from tainted spinach. Two employees *had* recently passed, but the institution said they had died from "sleeping sickness." The San simply couldn't have people thinking that their health food was killing people. And they really couldn't have people finding out that their spinach came from a cannery in California because they routinely touted the purity of their food—all of which was said to be grown, prepared, and processed on the grounds.

Questionable deaths aside, the San was the place to be at the turn of the century, and Dr. Kellogg was a bonafide celebrity. He was a best-selling author, a medical celebrity, a public health expert and a highly sought-after motivational speaker. His devout followers were referred to as "Battle Freaks." Dr. Kellogg oversaw operations at the San and its associated publishing company, both of which were owned by the Seventh-day Adventists, and he also co-owned two health food companies. But not everyone was a fan of Dr. Kellogg. Modern medical professionals hated him. They accused him of practicing dangerous, irregular medicine, which was honestly laughable. While his practices were definitely irregular, they were no more dangerous than the traditional treatments of the time. In the late 1800s, the life expectancy of men was just thirty-eight years, and the life expectancy of women was forty years. It was a well-known fact back then that one of the best things you could do for your health was not seek medical treatment. Dyspepsia, or indigestion, was treated with mercury. Opium was used for pain management. Strychnine and arsenic were used to get the blood pumping again in people with weak hearts. And God forbid a person suffer from inflammation of any kind. The treatment? Bloodletting, or the draining of blood from the body to relieve pain and inflammation.

The Battle Creek Sanitarium. *Courtesy of Erica Cooper, 2020.*

Another opposition to Dr. Kellogg came from an unexpected source—Mother White. She had paid for him to go to medical school and handed him the key to her health institute, and he'd made such a success out of it that the San was a worldwide spectacle. And he got all of the glory. Mother White was reportedly not pleased that the doctor had turned her modest establishment into what she considered a resort hotel. Dr. Kellogg, on the other hand, was frustrated by the restrictions the church put on him. He was an idea man, constantly thinking of new things he wanted to do, ways to expand and improve the San. But all of that took money, and therefore, he had to go through the church for approval. Most of his ideas were shot down immediately.

So, Dr. Kellogg, ever the problem solver, came up with a plan. The original charter for the wellness institute was only good for thirty years, and the good doctor knew this. In 1897, when that charter expired, a court order naturally made Dr. Kellogg, the facility's director and superintendent, the receiver. He formed a new organization, the Michigan Sanitarium and Benevolent Association, and carefully crafted every word of the charter, being sure to designate the San as a nonprofit and benevolent corporation. This designation required the new organization, by state law, to be nondenominational. When a public auction was held to sell off the old

The main entrance of the Battle Creek Sanitarium. *Courtesy of Erica Cooper, 2020.*

corporation's assets and property, the only bidder was the new corporation, Dr. Kellogg's corporation, which was nondenominational. So, the San became a private, distinct, independent entity, no longer officially part of the Seventh-day Adventist Church.

The Whites, understandably, were furious with Dr. Kellogg. Despite the fact that he continued to run the San in their image, based on the principles their church instilled in him as a young boy, Mother White turned on him. The resulting feud was so vicious that there would be no winners. And much of what was lost could never be recovered.

THINGS WE LOST IN THE FIRE

On February 18, 1902, Dr. Kellogg was on a train headed for home following a lecture series in California. Just before midnight, the train stopped at Chicago's Central Station. Dr. Kellogg got off to walk around and stretch his legs for a bit. He was approached by a reporter, which was not unusual—at first. Battle Creek is less than a couple hundred miles from Chicago, so Dr. Kellogg's celebrity was well known in the Windy City.

"Dr. Kellogg," the reporter asked anxiously, "are you going to rebuild?" A bit confused, the doctor responded, "Rebuild what?" The reporter was stunned, faced with the unenviable task of breaking the news to Dr. Kellogg. "Don't you know that the sanitarium burned down last night?"

Less than twenty-four hours earlier, night watchman William Hall was making his rounds at the San when he discovered a fire raging in the pharmacy's basement. At approximately 3:30 a.m. on February 18, he sounded the alarm of Battle Creek Fire Station No. 2.

Firefighters were on the scene within minutes, but flames were already exploding from the windows of the pharmacy and an attached bathhouse. They extinguished the fire at the small building quickly, but as they began to roll up their hoses and put their equipment away, they made a horrifying discovery. Just after 4:00 a.m., the ground began to rumble, and firefighters found themselves waist-deep in warm earth. The ground beneath their feet was literally melting, because the fire wasn't contained to the pharmacy building. It was in the tunnels underground. How do you fight an underground fire? You don't.

The Battle Creek Sanitarium ablaze, circa 1902. *Courtesy of the Willard Library Historical Collection.*

There were 307 guests at the San when it began to burn, many of them disabled and in wheelchairs. The staff worked calmly and quickly to get everyone out safely, and they did a phenomenal job—with one exception. Eighty-six-year-old Abner Case of Bath, New York, was asleep in his fourth-floor suite, along with his wife and daughter, when the fire broke out. He was being treated for chronic dyspepsia, or indigestion. The fire awoke Mrs. Case and her daughter, and they tried in vain to stir Mr. Case. He awoke disoriented, and didn't quite grasp the severity of the situation. When his wife told him they had to go, he refused, insisting instead that he needed to kneel beside the bed to pray. As the fire roared closer, Mrs. Case and her daughter made the heartbreaking decision to leave Mr. Case behind. Once outside, both women were hysterical. Staff doctor Howard Rand ran back inside in a last, desperate attempt to save Mr. Case. He found the confused man and led him to an exit door, but right on the precipice of safety, Mr. Case ran back into the fire, presumably to retrieve the bag full of cash that was still in his room. He was never seen again. A single human bone, a fragment of Mr. Case's humorous bone, was found by San staff a few weeks later.

Aside from the death of Abner Case, injuries were few. Mrs. H.C. McDaniels broke her leg after jumping from a sixth-floor window to escape the flames. She landed on the rooftop of an adjoining building and was saved by firefighter Laverne Fonda, who threw Mrs. McDaniels over his shoulder and slid over the edge of the roof to an awaiting ladder, delivering her to safety. He then went back and rescued Mr. McDaniels as well. Three firefighters were injured in the blaze, but none too seriously. The fire raged for hours and was seen as far away as Kalamazoo. In the light of day, the devastation was breathtaking. Nothing larger than a ten-foot-tall section of wall here or there remained standing. It was all gone.

When he was told of the fire by a reporter in Chicago, Dr. Kellogg remained stoic. "We will rebuild everything!" he confidently assured the man. When he returned to his seat on the train, he collapsed and could barely hold back his tears. He later said he felt like his best friend had died. His life's work was gone. But by the time his train pulled into the Battle Creek Station, Dr. Kellogg had already drawn up plans for a new building—a bigger, better, fireproof version of the San. Before he could look to the future, though, the elephant in the room had to be addressed. What caused the fire that destroyed the Battle Creek Sanitarium?

Partly owing to some questionable public statements he made following the fire, there were those who believed Dr. Kellogg himself was behind the fire. He once said, "Deep down in my heart, I am glad the building has burned because now we will build a better one." Another time, he said, "I have been longing for a better building, but I assure you that I didn't set the old building on fire." The prevailing theory, though, was that Mother White and her Seventh-day Adventists were responsible for the fires—fires, plural. The sanitarium wasn't the first of Dr. Kellogg's buildings to burn, and it would not be the last.

While a rift had been festering between Dr. Kellogg and Mother White for years, it solidified into a full-blown feud when he stole the San away from the church in 1897. A year later, on July 19, 1898, the Sanitarium Health Food Company owned by Dr. Kellogg burned to the ground under suspicious circumstances. Almost exactly two years after that, on July 21, 1900, the Sanitas Food Company, owned by the doctor and his brother Will, was destroyed by a fire of unknown origin. After the San itself burned, the eye of suspicion fell heavily on Mother White and her devout followers.

Onlookers crowd the streets as the remains of the *Review and Herald* building smolder. *Courtesy of the Willard Library Historical Collection.*

So when the offices of the *Review and Herald* Publishing House, which was owned by the Seventh-day Adventists but operated by Dr. Kellogg, burned to the ground just ten months after the San, it became a forgone conclusion that Mother White was to blame.

She had long voiced her opinion that the San was getting too big for its britches and becoming less God-like. The same was happening with the *Review and Herald* Publishing House. What started out as a means for Mother White to publish her magazines and pamphlets had become the largest publishing house in Michigan, responsible for publishing, among other things, all of Dr. Kellogg's books. *The Living Temple*, which was released just months before the publishing house burned, was his most inflammatory work yet, and it resulted in accusations of heresy. The fact that he used the Seventh-day Adventists publishing house to print it enraged Mother White. And then, a few months later, the *Review and Herald* building was gone. The very day of the fire, coincidentally, the fire inspector had gone through and inspected the building from top to bottom and found no violations or fire hazards.

Another possible motive for the fires—if they were indeed set by Mother White and her followers—was White's belief that God did not mean for her people to settle in Battle Creek. As early as 1882, she spoke of a vision in which God warned her and her followers to scatter. She was worried that Battle Creek was turning into a Vatican City for Seventh-day Adventists, and it kind of was. The church's headquarters and its two largest enterprises, the San and the *Review and Herald*, were all located in Battle Creek. Mother White herself had left Battle Creek following her husband's death in 1881 and settled in California around 1888. When the San burned, she suggested rebuilding in a different state, but Dr. Kellogg had veto power. When the *Review and Herald* burned, she relocated the publishing house to Washington, D.C. And with her gone, the San out from under the church's thumb, and the publishing house gone, the Seventh-day Adventist headquarters were relocated to Maryland. So the fires definitely helped her to achieve her goal of scattering her people.

The most damning evidence, however, was a statement she made following the fire at the *Review and Herald*, when even some of her own followers began to question her. She expressed sadness over the loss of yet another Seventh-day Adventist institution but said, "I have seen an angel standing with a sword as of fire stretched over Battle Creek. It seemed as if this sword of flame were turning first in one way and then another. Disaster seemed to follow disaster because God was dishonored by the devising of men to exalt and glorify themselves." It wasn't hard for her followers to guess what man, specifically, she was referring to.

The matter of pride also played a role in Mother White's animosity toward Dr. Kellogg. She was the founder of the Seventh-day Adventist Church, but many of her followers had begun to subscribe to Dr. Kellogg's religion of biologic living instead. She opened her publishing company in Battle Creek to spread her beliefs to the masses, but it was being used to pump out the doctor's worldwide best-sellers, the content of which she vehemently disagreed with. The idea of a wellness institute had come to her in a vision, and Dr. Kellogg had taken it and turned it into something else entirely. She was no longer the star of the show—he was. It was widely reported that she told followers, "Those buildings will burn. Dr. Kellogg has an imperious will that needs to be broken." The buildings did burn, but Dr. Kellogg's will was not broken.

Immediately after arriving back in Battle Creek following the fire at the San, Dr. Kellogg called an emergency meeting and unveiled his plans to rebuild to the church and local officials. The church balked at the plan and the price tag that came with it. They refused to fund the new facility. But technically, the church didn't own the San any longer—not legally. The church and the San were still heavily intertwined, but officially, they were separate entities. So the church had no say in the future of the San. They could withhold funding, and they did, but Dr. Kellogg had the autonomy to seek alternate funding sources. So that's what he did. The San had the power to make or break a community, so there were a plethora of other cities that wanted to house the new sanitarium and were willing to put up the capital to make it happen. When faced with the possibility of losing the San and the thousands of tourists it brought to town on a monthly basis, the city of Battle Creek put its money where its mouth was and facilitated loans and donations to help Dr. Kellogg rebuild.

But before the new sanitarium could even open its doors, tragedy struck again. On May 18, 1903, the stables at the new facility were set ablaze, killing thirteen horses and one charity patient. Less than two weeks later, on May 31, 1903, the new and improved Battle Creek Sanitarium opened to the public.

If the original sanitarium was a strange place, the upgraded version was like something out of a fever dream. It was basically a self-contained city. Made of brick and stone with marble and concrete flooring, Dr. Kellogg boasted that the new facility was "the only absolutely fireproof institution of this sort in the world." The six-story, state-of-the-art building

The Battle Creek Sanitarium. *Courtesy of Erica Cooper, 2020.*

Main Lobby, Battle Creek Sanitarium, Battle Creek, Mich.—8

The main lobby at the San. *Courtesy of the Willard Library Historical Collection.*

was composed of four hundred guest rooms and suites—the north wing for men, and the south wing for women. The treatment rooms on the fifth and sixth floors were equipped to treat more than one thousand patients per day.

There were three treatment wings that sprouted from the back of the building like spikes; one was a gymnasium with mechanical horses and camels, mechanical kneading machines meant to "stimulate the crippled colon," different varieties of vibrating machines, and a plethora of the mad doctor's various contraptions. One was a bathhouse composed of white-tiled pools and baths of all sorts, and the other was a state-of-the-art sanctum santorum, or enema room. The new sanitarium offered over two hundred different water treatments, including sprays, douches, enemas, and baths. A brass band played music throughout every meal, and every evening, there was a grand march on the roof, where guests did aerobics and calisthenics. Everything at the San was top-of-the-line, including the elaborate system Dr. Kellogg created for purifying and recirculating air, and the year-round indoor palm garden filled with exotic birds and butterflies from the doctor's own personal collection. Out of the ashes rose something grander than anyone could have envisioned when Mother White first opened the Western Health Reform Institute in 1867. But the city wasn't finished burning yet. The worst was still to come.

The men's lounge at the San. *Courtesy of the Willard Library Historical Collection.*

The women's lounge at the San. *Courtesy of the Willard Library Historical Collection.*

The Haskell Home for Orphans. *Courtesy of the Willard Library Historical Collection.*

On November 10, 1907, after over a decade of feuding, Dr. Kellogg was officially excommunicated from the Seventh-day Adventist Church, a move he'd seen coming for years. It was a weight off his shoulders, freeing him from the shackles of what he viewed as an authoritarian religion. He accused the church of trying to "cripple and destroy the Battle Creek Sanitarium and every work with which I am connected."

Dr. Kellogg loved children, clearly, which was why he fostered and adopted several dozen of them over the years. By the 1880s, he was being asked to take in children at such a rate that he knew there was a need for an orphanage in Battle Creek. Caroline Haskell, a widow from Indiana who was staying at the San, donated $30,000 to build an orphanage in Battle Creek on the condition that it be named after her late husband and designated as a nondenominational institution open to all races.

The Haskell Home for Orphans was dedicated on January 25, 1894. It, like the San and the *Review and Herald*, was run by the Seventh-day Adventist Church. But when the doctor was excommunicated, so was the orphanage. Dr. Kellogg kept it running, though, much to Mother White's dismay.

The gothic-style mansion was built to accommodate 150 orphans, but luckily, there were only 37 children staying at the orphanage the night it went up in flames. In the early morning hours of February 5, 1909, fifteen-year-old Mary Armstrong, who was staying at the Haskell Home with 5 of her 12 siblings, awoke to find the girls' dormitory filled with smoke. She could hear fire crackling from the floor below. With the stairs and fire escape both blocked by flames, Mary broke a window on the third floor. Down on the ground, she saw her twelve-year-old brother, James, who had climbed up onto a shed and begun yelling for the girls to jump down to him. Mary picked up her five-year-old sister, Pearl, and tossed her out the window. James caught her and helped her to safety. More children followed. Once the younger girls were safe, the bigger girls began to jump. James could no longer catch them, but he helped them to land safely, preventing broken bones for many of them.

Mary kept order in the girls' dormitory and helped her bunkmates to safety until she was overcome by smoke and fire. She leapt from the window, missed the shed, and hit the ground. She was left with serious injuries to her face and head, including temporary blindness caused by severe blistering. Unfortunately, Mary wasn't able to help everyone out before she had to jump.

Twelve-year-old Cecil Coutant, who had lived at the orphanage since she was five, shook with terror as she stood in the window following Mary's dangerous fall. "I'm afraid!" she shrieked, before disappearing from the window into the inferno as the floor beneath her collapsed, killing both her and fourteen-year-old Lena McKay of Battle Creek.

The Haskell Home for Orphans ablaze. *Courtesy of the Willard Library Historical Collection.*

Lena was only a temporary guest at the Haskell Home. Her family was on vacation in Florida, and she'd been left behind so doctors could tend to an injured hand.

Superintendent Rodney Owen and his wife, Sarah, lived at the Haskell Home with the children. When they awoke to the presence of smoke, Rodney ran into the kitchen, hoping the fire was contained and manageable, while Sarah gathered up a group of young boys and led them toward safety as they clung to her dress. Just as they reached the exit, she remembered that the orphanage had just taken in a six-week-old baby who was trapped in his crib. The smallest boys refused to leave her, so with them still hanging onto her, she made her way back inside. She rescued baby Donald, then ran down a burning staircase with two little boys trailing behind her. Only once she was outside safely and able to take a head count did she realize that one was still missing—eight-year-old George Goodenow, the only Black child at the orphanage, recently arrived from Chattanooga, Tennessee. No one recalled seeing him in the commotion, so it was thought that he either didn't wake up or perished trying to find his own way out.

The remains of Cecil, Lena and little George were all buried in the same grave at the Haskell Home Cemetery in Battle Creek. The source of the fire that took their lives was never determined. Initially, officials conceded that it was likely caused by arson, which was Dr. Kellogg's belief as well. But just a few days later, officials declared that there would be no investigation because they had no reason to believe it was anything other than a horrific accident.

However, according to the February 6, 1909 edition of the *Detroit Free Press*, the Haskell Home blaze was the twelfth fire of a structure previously owned by or connected to the Seventh-day Adventists in as many years. Of those fires, eight were of unknown origin; two were determined to be arson, and two were ruled accidental. A total of five people perished in the West End Fires, as they became known: the three children at the orphanage, Abner Case in the first sanitarium fire, and the patient killed in the stable fire at the new sanitarium. Fire Chief Weeks, who unsuccessfully fought all of the West End fires, once told the church, "There is something strange about your SDA fires." Something strange indeed.

Whether it was Mother White and her followers or just a series of unfortunate coincidences, fire seemed to have it out for Dr. Kellogg. But he never let the tragedies overcome him. It was something else entirely that brought him to his knees. When he rebuilt the San after the fire, he overextended himself with loans and promissory notes, believing that his clients, the millionaires and twentieth-century elite, would always be swimming in cash. But the stock market crash of 1929 hit his clientele particularly hard, and the San went bankrupt in 1933. At least there was still the cereal empire.

THE CEREAL KING

D r. John Harvey Kellogg was larger than life. His accomplishments were celebrated worldwide, and for a time, it seemed that everything he touched turned to gold. While the doctor was always quick to accept accolades for his successes, he rarely, if ever, shared the credit as he should have. Because without his younger brother Will Keith Kellogg, there would have been no Dr. Kellogg, no sanitarium, and no Kellogg Company.

Will was born on April 7, 1860, the youngest son of John Preston and Ann Janette Kellogg. He was eight years Dr. Kellogg's junior, so the family was already living in Battle Creek and heavily involved with the Seventh-day Adventist Church by the time Will came on the scene. Although he and the doctor grew up in the same household, their upbringings couldn't have been more different.

Will's mother, Ann, was John Sr.'s second wife. John Sr. and his first wife, Mary, had five children together. While the children were still very young, Mary contracted tuberculosis and was bedridden. During this time, she and John hired the teenage daughter of a local blacksmith to help out with the house and children. Her name was Ann Janette Stanley.

On September 27, 1841, just days before her thirtieth birthday, Mary succumbed to tuberculosis, leaving her thirty-five-year-old husband a widower. Men did not raise children on their own in the 1800s, and certainly not five of them at once. If the Kellogg family had any chance of making it, the children needed a new mother. So John Sr. went out and found them one.

On March 29, 1842, six months after his wife's death, John Sr. hitched his horses to his wagon in the early morning hours and told his children, "I expect to bring someone home with me." He returned later that evening, and the children were ecstatic to see their former nanny, Ann. As they hugged her and fussed over her, John Sr. announced, "You must not call her Ann. You must call her mother, for she is your mother now."

And that was that. Ann raised John Sr.'s children as if they were her own, and then she gave birth to twelve more. By the time Will was born, Dr. Kellogg (who was still just John Harvey at the time) had solidly earned the title of momma's boy. As such, there wasn't any room for Will. He grew up feeling unloved and unworthy. While all of the Kellogg children had different experiences with their parents, the one thing they agreed on was that their father was very reserved and never paid any of them much mind. With the exception of her affection for her favorite son, their mother was much the same way. At the same time, Mr. and Mrs. Kellogg did good things in the world. They were station agents for Battle Creek's Underground Railroad. The danger they put themselves in to help others left a lasting impression on all of their children. They were good, charitable, philanthropic citizens, and they worked hard to support their family. They just had difficulty showing love outwardly to the people who needed to see it the most.

Will and his older brother were polar opposites. Whereas John Harvey was charismatic and vivacious, funny and quick-witted, Will was quiet and socially awkward. He later described himself as a miserable child who never learned to play. He hated his older brother. The future doctor was verbally and physically abusive to Will, always picking on him and tattling on him. Will also hated school. He was slow to read, and his teachers and parents thought he was dimwitted. What Will would discover at the age of twenty, when he had his first eye test, was that he wasn't dumb at all; he was just severely nearsighted. So it wasn't that he couldn't read, it was that he couldn't see. And once he could see, he soared.

Will grew up working in the family broom factory along with his siblings. When he was eighteen, he moved to Texas to work at a broom factory there, but he returned to Battle Creek the following year. In 1880, when he was twenty, Will met, fell in love with, and married a young woman by the name of Ella Osborn-Davis. The couple was married on November 3, 1880, after a whirlwind courtship. They bought a modest house on Champion Street not far from the San, where Will had recently taken a job, and they set about raising a family. Their first child, a son named Karl, was born in 1881.

Their second son, John, was born in 1883. Their third son, W.K. Jr., was born in 1885, but he died just a few years later at the age of four. Their only daughter, Elizabeth, was born in 1888, and their youngest child, Irving, was born in 1894, but he did not live to see his first birthday.

Will wasn't as extreme as his eccentric older brother and led a more conventional life. Much like his parents, he wasn't warm or affectionate, but he took good care of his family. He wasn't a devout Christian and didn't often attend church, but he prayed every night before bed. He didn't follow a strict diet; he was mindful of what he ate, but he still ate meat and indulged in sweets. He wasn't quite as fanatical about animals as his brother, but he did love horses. One of his few joys as a child was spending time with his favorite horse, Old Spot. One day, when he was very young, he returned home from school only to find out that his father had sold the horse to a neighbor. He never recovered from that loss, so when he was older and had the money, he bought himself a horse—several horses, actually. He ran an eight-hundred-acre Arabian horse ranch in California that was one of the finest in the country.

The same year Will met and married Ella Osborn-Davis, who went by "Puss," he also started working at the San as his brother's assistant. Even in their twenties, the brothers still didn't get along (and never would), but the doctor trusted his brother, so he relied on him for everything. He put Will in charge of the *Review and Herald* Publishing Company and the day-to-day operations at the San. The doctor was the showman, but Will was the one running the show.

Still, the doctor never gave Will a title—not "vice president of operations" or "junior partner," nothing. Will worked seven years before he was granted his first vacation, and was paid just nine dollars a week, even though he worked over one hundred hours most weeks. He didn't even get an office of his own until he'd been at the San for over a decade, and that was little more than a glorified utility closet.

Despite everything Will did for his brother, Dr. Kellogg enjoyed humiliating him, just as he had when they were children. Every day, Will shined the doctor's shoes and trimmed his beard. Dr. Kellogg often rode a bicycle around the San's campus and would make Will run along beside him and dictate his thoughts. He forced Will to join him in the bathroom for his five-times-daily bowel movements so that Will could write down his ideas as they came to him. For the thousands of people who Dr. Kellogg tortured over the years with his strange contraptions and strict regimens, he tortured his brother most of all. Will worked nights, weekends, and holidays. He was constantly at the doctor's beck and call. The strangest thing is that through all of this, Will absolutely hated his brother, so he wasn't doing any of it out of brotherly love. But he stayed. For over twenty years, he did Dr. Kellogg's bidding for him.

When Dr. Kellogg had his dream of flaked cereal, it was Will who he trusted to help make it happen. No one disputes that flaked cereal was Dr. Kellogg's idea, but how that idea was brought to fruition is another matter, as all parties involved told different stories.

The story Dr. Kellogg told was simple and very self-serving. He said that one night, around 3:00 a.m., he was awakened by a phone call from a patient. He took the call, and as he was getting ready to go back to bed, he remembered that he'd been dreaming of making flaked cereal. So, the next morning, he got up, boiled some wheat, ran it through his wife's rolling machine, scraped it off the rollers with a knife and baked it in the oven. Viola! Wheat flakes, which would later become the much more popular corn flakes, followed by the even more popular frosted flakes.

According to Ella Kellogg, the doctor's wife, she and her husband had been trying to come up with a flaked cereal recipe for a while and couldn't quite get it right. It was she who suggested that the dough be rolled out as thin as possible, and it was also she who suggested John design a set of rollers that turned via crank to accomplish this. She said that one day, while they were working on their wheat flake recipe, the doctor was called away from the house to treat a patient at the San. He left a batch of dough out while he was gone, and when he returned the next day, it had gone stale. He fed it through the rollers anyway, simply to see what would happen, and the flakes came out perfectly, just as he'd seen them in his dream.

Will's version of how flaked cereal was invented is completely different. According to him, the invention was a 50/50 partnership between the two brothers, and Ella Kellogg played no role in it—not even the offering up of her kitchen. Will said the first successful batch of flaked cereal was created in the San's kitchen. His story goes like this: One Friday night, after a long week of work, the two brothers were working in the kitchen on their flaked cereal recipe, and they decided to give up right in the middle of a batch to go home to get some rest. Will put the dough in a container so they could pick back up where they left off. The brothers returned to the kitchen two days later, and when they took the dough from its container, they discovered it was a bit moldy. They put it through the rollers and baked it anyway, and it came out as perfectly crispy flakes, if not a little green.

Whatever story is true, wheat flakes were born in the late summer of 1894. Corn flakes soon followed. A year later, the cereal was served at the

San for the first time. The guests loved it. While Dr. Kellogg was simply happy to add another health food to the San's menu, Will, by then a successful businessman, saw the true potential of their creation. Flaked cereal could make them millions if they added ingredients like sugar and malt, engaged in a mass marketing campaign, and went all-in on the breakfast food business. But Dr. Kellogg wanted none of that. He was a serious doctor (who wore a cockatoo on his shoulder), running a serious wellness retreat (where grown adults had to sing a song about chewing before every meal), and he worried that going into the breakfast food business on a wider scale would tarnish his reputation. Oddly, he wasn't worried about his overt racism or the mutilation of children's genitals affecting his legacy. Per Dr. Kellogg's orders, corn flakes were marketed as a health food only at first. Meanwhile, word got out that he'd found a way to turn sixty cents worth of wheat into twelve dollars' worth of gold. And the wolves descended. A "cereal gold rush" of sorts began in Battle Creek. Over one hundred cereal companies popped up in the city between 1888 and 1905.

One of the most successful copycats was Charley Post, a thirty-six-year-old failed businessman who was treated at the San for chronic pain and autointoxication. He suffered from severe anxiety and depression and was prone to nervous breakdowns. Wheelchair-bound and in very poor health, Post was given a tour of the San's kitchens and treated to a demonstration of the cereal-making process, much to Will's chagrin.

Predictably, Post left the San, bought himself a plot of land in Battle Creek, and began stealing all of the Kelloggs' ideas. He first tried to open his own wellness sanitarium, but that was a huge failure. He then copied several of the San's recipes and marketed them as his own under the Postum Cereal Company Brand, now known as Post Foods. Post also launched a successful advertisement campaign that he called, "The Road to Wellville," which was later the name of a satirical book and subsequent movie about the cereal boom in Battle Creek.

At first, Dr. Kellogg didn't seem to mind too much that Post was stealing his ideas, but it drove Will crazy. Everyone was making money off of the Kelloggs' creations except for the Kelloggs. And this was the catalyst for Will finally breaking free from his brother—the pursuit of a cereal fortune. All of his ill-gotten gains couldn't save Charley Post, though, and on May 9, 1914, he sat down in his favorite chair, put a shotgun in his mouth, and pulled the trigger with his toe. He died just shy of his sixtieth birthday. The Kelloggs did not mourn him.

In 1905, after over twenty years of faithful service to his older brother, Will made the decision to leave the San and offered to take the cereal business with him. His timing was perfect. Dr. Kellogg was in danger of defaulting on the loans he'd taken out to rebuild the San after the fire, and he didn't see a whole lot of value in the cereal business once there were a hundred other companies in Battle Creek making the same thing. So he let it go pretty easily, which was quite honestly one of the wilder things he ever did.

On February 19, 1906, Will Kellogg founded the Battle Creek Toasted Corn Flake Company, which later became the Kellogg's Toasted Corn Flake Company and is now simply known as the Kellogg Company. He revolutionized the mass production and marketing of food and blew all of his imposters out of the water. Soon, his factories were producing 120,000 boxes of corn flakes per day. But it wasn't all smooth sailing. On July 4, 1907, like many of the other buildings owned by the Kelloggs, Will's cereal factory burned to the ground under suspicious circumstances. Like his brother, Will rebuilt bigger and better. But the next blow came from much closer to home.

If John Harvey Kellogg was one of the most successful, beloved doctors in the country (and he was), Will Keith Kellogg was one of the world's most successful industrialists—and that drove the doctor crazy. In 1908, the

Will's original Toasted Corn Flake Company. *Courtesy of the Willard Library Historical Collection.*

Will Kellogg at his cereal factory. *Courtesy of the W.K. Kellogg Foundation.*

year Will began operating under the name "Kellogg's Toasted Corn Flake Company," Dr. Kellogg began mass marketing breakfast cereal, the very thing he refused to allow Will to do for over a decade. And he didn't do it under his Sanitarium Foods label or through the Sanitas Food Company; no, he created yet a third health food company, Kellogg's Food Company of Battle Creek. But Will was already marketing breakfast cereal out of Battle Creek using the Kellogg name—a right he'd paid a lot of money for. And the town wasn't big enough for the both of them. Not only did Dr. Kellogg mirror his brother's company name, but his packaging was nearly identical to Will's, right down to the Kellogg signature on the box.

So in 1910, Will filed a lawsuit requesting a permanent injunction against his brother's use of the Kellogg name for the purpose of selling breakfast foods. The case went all the way to the Michigan Supreme Court and lasted for ten years. Their arguments were these: John claimed that he had invented corn flakes, which was true. He also claimed the he was the more famous of the two brothers and that his face was synonymous with the Kellogg name, which was also true. Will claimed that his brother had signed away his rights to corn flakes, which was true, and that, by 1920, when the case reached the Supreme Court, the Kellogg name was much more well-known for breakfast foods than it was for the San, which, again, was true. In the end, the courts sided with Will. The brothers, then in their sixties, rarely spoke again.

Will's star continued to soar. The Kellogg Company grew in ways he'd never imagined, and after decades of humiliating, thankless work, he was able to live out his golden years a rich man, raising his horses and enjoying his family—to the extent that a man who enjoys nothing can enjoy things.

The doctor, however, fell hard. He'd been excommunicated by the church, lost out on the Kellogg cereal fortune, was in failing health, and by the 1930s, he was in the final stages of losing the San. He'd had to step away from day-to-day operations due to health issues, and the doctors who took over had very different views on health and wellness. They ditched the vegan menu and brought back meat and processed foods, and they also began smoking indoors. The San was no longer a one-of-a-kind health and wellness retreat; it was just another hospital. Then came the receivership in 1933 and, finally, the sale of the facility to the U.S. government in 1942. During those final, difficult years, Dr. Kellogg reached out to his rich and successful younger brother several times under the guise of mending fences, but he always ended up asking Will to bail him out financially so he could salvage his hospital and reputation. Will would have none of it. In fact, he actively participated in the Seventh-day Adventists' attempt to buy back the San, which was ultimately unsuccessful.

Will's Battle Creek mansion. *Courtesy of Erica Cooper, 2020.*

The doctor's descent into madness continued, and his behavior became increasingly erratic. He began playing show-and-tell with his stool samples. He would take a container into the bathroom with him and emerge with a fresh stool, which he then forced his unfortunate companions to smell. He was very proud of his odorless poop. He took to exercising and going out in public virtually naked, wearing what amounted to little more than a loin cloth. Will was so angered and embarrassed by his brother's behavior that he tried to file an injunction to make Dr. Kellogg wear clothes in public. His lawyers, wisely, cautioned him against it.

The brothers last saw one another on October 3, 1942, when Dr. Kellogg once again asked Will for money to try to save the San. The meeting ended in a heated argument. A couple months later, on December 14, 1942, Dr. John Harvey Kellogg died from complications of pneumonia at the age of ninety-one, just nine years shy of his goal to live to be one hundred. Always one to follow in his brother's footsteps, cereal king Will Keith Kellogg also died at the age of ninety-one, on October 6, 1951. Following his death, Will's body was put on display at the Kellogg production factory for twenty-four hours, so employees could pay their respects.

Today, the Kellogg Company rakes in $13 billion in annual sales, primarily through selling ridiculously unhealthy foods that would have both the doctor and his brother rolling in their graves. And for all of the strange contraptions and devices Dr. Kellogg invented to torment his patients, it was actually a simple utility knife from Will's cereal factory that resulted in one of the most brutal murders Battle Creek has ever seen.

THE WILDFLOWER

When cereal king Will Kellogg passed away on October 6, 1951, his death made headlines around the world, and the thousands of employees at his Kellogg Company in Battle Creek mourned him. Among them was thirty-two-year-old Daisy Zick, a popular, vivacious redhead who would soon make headlines of her own.

Daisy Marie Holmes was born on her family's farm on Mud Creek Road in Assyria Township, about ten miles north of Battle Creek, on February 5, 1919. Her sister Dorothy was born two years later. The Holmes girls attended a one-room schoolhouse during the day and helped out on the family farm at night. Daisy finished school through the eighth grade, which was around the time she met and fell in love with her neighbor Neville "Bill" King. The two were married soon after, on September 29, 1933. Daisy was fourteen; her husband was twenty-two. The young couple moved to Battle Creek, where Bill made good money working at the United Steel and Wire Company in town.

When Daisy was seventeen, she gave birth to her only child, a son, James. But life in the King household was not the happily ever after Daisy had hoped for. Her husband was terribly abusive, both physically and mentally. He berated Daisy, called her horrible names, hit her, kicked her, and once even broke her nose. The violence in the King household was so conspicuous that neighbors often complained. The day Bill threatened to kill Daisy, she took baby James, not yet a year old, and went back to the family farm on Mud Creek Road. But Daisy, then eighteen, was too young to file for divorce on her own in the eyes of the court. Her father had to do it for her. The divorce proceedings went quickly, and Bill was ordered to pay three dollars a week in child support. The adjustment was tough on everyone; Bill was still filled with all that rage, and Daisy and James were both young and vulnerable. But eventually, things settled down, and Bill faded into the background, his only role in his son's life the weekly checks he sent.

Shortly after her divorce, Daisy took a job at one of Battle Creek's many food companies, Nabisco. Her sister Dorothy worked at the nearby Western Biscuit Company, and the two girls, both still teenagers, decided to get an apartment together in the city. The drive from the farm to the factories wasn't terribly long, but most of the roads were dirt roads, and the trek was not an easy one. Or, at least, that was the reason Daisy gave when she made the decision to move to Battle Creek without her child. She left James, then a toddler, on the farm with her parents, only traveling the ten miles home to visit him on weekends.

In 1941, when the United States dove headfirst into World War II, the city of Battle Creek transformed seemingly overnight. The factories changed gears and began manufacturing food and other supplies for troops, and nearby Fort Custer became an active military training base. With an influx of men in uniform training, living, and working in Battle Creek, Daisy, along with many other single ladies in the area, became a party girl, going to dances and bars that were frequented by soldiers on a nightly basis. She had brief flings with a number of military men before she met Floyd Zick, a newly enlisted soldier in the United States Army. The two were married in 1942, when they were both twenty-three. Daisy's son, James, who was six at this point, was given a choice: he could move with his mother and stepfather to Battle Creek or stay with his grandparents on the farm where he'd spent most of his life. He chose to stay on the farm. After Floyd returned from the war, he took a job as a butcher at Fales Market in Battle Creek. Daisy took a job working the night shift at the Kellogg Company. Daisy and Floyd were an outgoing, fun-loving couple. Floyd was a jokester who liked to make people laugh, and Daisy was known for her kind heart and big smile. But they were both known for other things, too. Floyd was a heavy drinker, and Daisy had a wandering eye. Whether Daisy's infidelity was a result of her husband's alcoholism or vice versa remains to be seen, but as early as the 1950s, rumors began running rampant around town about Daisy and other men.

Tuesday, January 14, 1963, was a bitterly cold day in Battle Creek's Wattles Park neighborhood, where Daisy and Floyd Zick lived in a small, two-bedroom brick ranch home on Jono Road. The snow was six inches deep, with forecasters predicting an additional couple of inches by nightfall amid gusting winds. The temperature was right around zero degrees Fahrenheit at daybreak, but was expected to drop to seventeen below by the end of the day. It's the kind of weather that takes your breath away, that makes you not want to go outside unless absolutely necessary. Which is why the events that unfolded in the Zick household that day went unnoticed by neighbors.

Floyd Zick got up that morning, kissed his wife goodbye, and left for work around 7:45 a.m. Daisy was working the afternoon shift at Kellogg, so she didn't leave until later in the day. Floyd called home at 9:00 a.m., like he did every day, to make sure Daisy was awake and getting ready for work. She told him she was just about to hop in the bath, then go meet a friend for coffee before work. They said their goodbyes, and Floyd returned to the business of butchering giant slabs of meat for sale.

Around 12:30 p.m., Floyd got a call at work from Daisy's friend and coworker Audrey Heminger. The two women were supposed to meet for coffee before their shift, but Daisy never showed. She was also late for work and hadn't called in, which was very unlike her. And she wasn't answering the phone at home, either. Something was wrong.

Floyd left work immediately to go home and check on his wife. During his four-mile drive, he wondered if maybe her car had broken down due to the bitter cold. About halfway home, Floyd spotted Daisy's white 1959 Pontiac Bonneville on the shoulder of Evanston Road, but there was no sign of Daisy. Worried she might have broken down and set off on foot for help, he decided to see if the car would start. Daisy's keys weren't in the ignition, so he used his spare set to turn the car on. It started just fine. In his haste, Floyd failed to notice the blood smeared on both the interior and exterior of Daisy's car.

Floyd got back into his car and drove the last couple of miles home. When he arrived, he found the door to Daisy's side of the garage door open, which immediately struck him as odd. Everything about the situation was odd. Daisy was a very conscientious person. She was punctual and kept an immaculate home. So for her to miss a coffee date and her shift at work, and to leave her car on the side of the road and the garage door open was extremely out of character. Floyd had a sinking feeling that something awful had happened to his wife. That feeling only solidified as he approached the house. There was a small breezeway between the garage and the house. The door to the breezeway was often left unlocked, but the door that led into the kitchen was always locked, even when Daisy was home. Floyd found the door to the kitchen not only unlocked, but also slightly ajar. He called out for his wife but got no response.

Once inside the home, Floyd began to panic. The kitchen rug was bunched up against the counter as if someone had been running and skidded into it. Daisy's half-packed lunch was on the table, along with her work shoes. But if she'd never left for work—and she clearly hadn't—how did her car wind up over on Evanston Road?

Floyd headed for the master bedroom, hoping that Daisy had maybe fallen suddenly ill and gone back to bed. But she wasn't there. What he found instead was their white bedspread in disarray, splattered with blood. The contents of Daisy's purse had been dumped onto the floor, and her purse was sitting upright on the floor at the end of the bed. Her wallet was on the bed. Her twenty-six-dollar paycheck was still inside, but the forty-five dollars in cash that Floyd had given her to deposit at the bank that morning was missing. Floyd raced back toward the kitchen to call for help, but the phone line had been cut. Someone had been in the house and was maybe still there. But who? The living room appeared undisturbed, as did the bathroom. There was only one place left to check—the spare bedroom.

The first thing Floyd noticed when he opened the door was that the heavy hi-fi cabinet was pushed out from the wall, as if someone was maybe trying to hide behind it or perhaps push it toward the door as a barricade. Then he saw the blood, smeared and splattered along the wall. He followed the trail of blood to the floor, where he saw Daisy's black-and-gold slippers sticking out from behind the bed. She was on her back, her legs bent into an unnatural position. Her hands were bound behind her, and she was so covered in blood that Floyd couldn't make out her features. But he knew it was her. When he reached out to touch her, she was cold.

Floyd ran to the basement, where there was a second telephone. Instead of calling the police, he called Fale's Market, where he worked. He told his assistant manager that Daisy had been shot and asked him to call the police. This sounds like an odd detail, but in 1963, there was no 911. Floyd likely didn't have the number to the police memorized, so in his panic, he called a number he knew by heart instead.

At 1:15 p.m., Lowell McDonald, the assistant manager of Fale's Market, placed a call to the Michigan State Police post in Battle Creek to report a murder at 100 Jono Road in Wattles Park. While Lowell was on the phone with the police, Floyd was on the phone with Daisy's friend Audrey, the one who had alerted him that something was wrong. As the shocking news that forty-three-year-old Daisy Zick had been murdered spread throughout the

Kellogg factory like wildfire, Floyd Zick sat quietly beside his wife's body for fifteen minutes, waiting for police to arrive.

The Michigan State Police and the Calhoun County Sheriff's Office worked the case together. Detective Charlie Conn from the state police and Undersheriff Wayne Fitch from Calhoun County were assigned as the lead investigators. They determined that Daisy wasn't shot like Floyd had assumed, but bludgeoned and stabbed at least twenty times. The suspected murder weapon was a spoilage knife, identical to the ones used at the Kellogg factory to open boxes. The knife was found in the Zicks' sink, still spotted with blood.

Investigators determined that sometime after 10:00 a.m., someone entered the Zick home through the breezeway door. Daisy then opened the interior door to allow the intruder inside the house, likely because she knew the person. The point of entry was corroborated by a statement one of Daisy's neighbors gave to police. Mrs. George DeFrance said that she'd gone out to get her mail a little after 10:00 a.m. and saw a man standing at the breezeway door of the Zick home. He was jumping up and down, likely his body's way of fighting off the biting cold. He had dark hair, was of medium height, and was wearing a dark blue jacket. It was not uncommon for strange men to be spotted at the Zick home after Floyd had left for work, so Mrs. DeFrance thought nothing of it. About twenty minutes later, while she was letting her dog out, Mrs. DeFrance noticed that the garage door at the Zick place was wide open and that Daisy's car was gone. This did strike her as odd, but not odd enough to alert authorities.

Authorities surmised that Daisy was in her bedroom getting ready for work when she heard a knock at the door, and unwittingly let a murderer into her home. Some sort of confrontation occurred in the kitchen, and when Daisy tried to run, she was struck from behind with a blunt object. Dazed, she went for the phone, but her attacker severed the phone cord, likely with the same blade that was used to kill Daisy moments later. She fled to her bedroom, and her attacker followed. He used the sash from Daisy's robe to bind her hands behind her back and stabbed her at least once in the master bedroom, which was why there was blood on the bedspread.

Daisy somehow escaped and ran to the spare bedroom. She pulled the hi-fi cabinet from the wall in an attempt to either hide behind it or push it up against the door so her attacker couldn't get in. But the assailant made it into the bedroom before Daisy was able to block the door. So she fought—hard. She had a number of defensive wounds to her arms, broken ribs and several of her immaculate fingernails were torn and ripped. In the end, it wasn't enough. After Daisy was dead, her killer rifled through her purse, either as an afterthought or in an attempt to make the murder look like a robbery gone wrong. They took her keys and what little cash she had, then fled in her car before ditching it a couple miles away.

Due to the brutality of Daisy's murder, investigators determined it was likely a crime of passion. When a woman is murdered, there's a common phrase in the true crime world: "The husband did it." Not only did Daisy have a husband she was being unfaithful to and an ex-husband who'd been violent and abusive toward her, she also had a boyfriend. For over two years, she'd been openly dating Ray Mercer, her coworker at the Kellogg factory. Ray was one of the last people to speak to Daisy that morning. He called her from work shortly after 9:00 a.m., after she'd gotten off the phone with Floyd. They talked for about fifteen minutes before exchanging "I love yous" and promising to see each other at work.

Daisy's ex-husband Neville "Bill" King was ruled out quickly. He and Daisy hadn't spoken in years, and there was no animosity there. He didn't care about her one way or another, certainly not enough to seek her out after decades of no contact and kill her. Her husband, Floyd, and boyfriend, Ray, had solid alibis: they were both at work. And they both passed polygraph tests with flying colors.

Investigators then turned their attention to Daisy's friend Audrey Heminger, the one Daisy was supposed to meet for coffee before work. Rumor had it that Daisy and Audrey, an attractive woman five years Daisy's junior, were more like frenemies than actual friends. It was said that the two women, who were both married, often competed for the affections of their male coworkers at Kellogg. Could Audrey have killed Daisy in a jealous rage? During intense questioning from the police, Audrey got upset and fled the interrogation in tears. She stopped cooperating after that.

The evidence collected from Daisy's home and car didn't amount to much. Investigators found a lone white button on the floor of the Zick home that didn't belong to Daisy or Floyd. There were yellow fibers on Daisy's person, about the home, and in her car that they believed likely came from a pair of yellow work gloves, much like the ones worn by Kellogg factory workers. They had the spoilage knife that was the suspected murder weapon, also believed to be from Kellogg. And there was a single fingerprint on the rearview mirror of Daisy's car that couldn't be attributed to anyone who had cause to be in Daisy's vehicle.

Multiple witnesses saw Daisy's murderer, though no one got a close enough look to be helpful. Her neighbor across the street, Mrs. DeFrance, saw a man at the house just before Daisy was killed. He was described as a white male, five feet, seven inches tall, 135 pounds, in his late twenties or early thirties, with dark hair. He was wearing a dark blue jacket and lighter blue pants.

Mailman William Newman Daily, who delivered mail to the Wattles Park neighborhood, said that just after 10:00 a.m., he saw a man walking down Michigan Avenue near the Zick home. The man was described as dark-complected, five feet, eight inches tall, 150 to 170 pounds, around forty years old, with black hair, wearing a black waist-length jacket. Normally, a man walking down the street wouldn't be an automatic suspect in a homicide case or even a detail that anyone would remember, but it was so cold that day, anyone out walking stood out like a sore thumb.

On the morning of Daisy's death, Sergeant Fred Ritchie of the Calhoun County Sheriff's Department was transporting a prisoner to the courthouse and was running behind schedule when he saw Daisy's car parked on the shoulder of Evanston Road. The cold weather had disabled vehicles all over the area, so he didn't think much of it—or of the man in the blue jacket walking away from the car.

Forty-nine-year-old Garrett Vander Meer was driving down Michigan Avenue around 11:00 a.m. on that fateful morning when he got held up in traffic behind a white Pontiac Bonneville that was driving erratically at a speed of about ten miles per hour. The car eventually pulled over on Evanston Road, and as Mr. Vander Meer passed, he got a closeup look at the driver. He described a good-sized, healthy looking, good looking fellow, a white male with a "kinda medium-sized face that wasn't real red." His face wasn't "skinny or puffed up," and his nose "wasn't a fat nose. It was more on the slim side." He appeared to be about five feet, eleven inches tall, even though he was sitting down, and he looked to be anywhere from thirty to thirty-five years old. His dark-brown hair was the most distinctive thing about him, Vander Meer said. He wore it puffed up in the front and sleeked back at the parts.

At a loss, investigators began focusing on the Kellogg factory, which had become known for its seedy subculture of sex, scandal, and all-around debauchery. It was common for married men to have "shop wives," as they called them, for married women to compete for the affections of their male colleagues, and for adulterous affairs to be carried out in the parking lot on lunch breaks or in dark corridors of the factory. While the day shift was said to more or less toe the line, the night shift, where Daisy started, was wild. They smoked, drank, played music and danced the night away while boxing up Froot Loops and Corn Pops. Daisy worked on the production line and sat at the end of a row so that anyone passing through the factory had to walk by her. The women's uniform at Kellogg was a form-fitting white dress, stockings, and white shoes. Daisy was one of the few women who spiced it up with makeup. She was beautiful, talkative, and had a smile for everyone who passed by her.

Over eighty men from the Kellogg factory were taken in for questioning, which was said to have broken up quite a few marriages. Given Daisy's reputation, if a man was questioned as a suspect, there had to be a reason. He must have been having an affair with her. Police questioned the wife of one Kellogg employee who had confronted Daisy a week before the murder and accused her of sleeping with her husband. They questioned Floyd Zick's longtime mistress—it seemed Daisy wasn't the only one who didn't respect the sanctity of her marriage. They investigated the prank calls Daisy and Floyd had been getting at home and at work in the months before the murder, calls that continued even after Daisy's death. Every single lead was a dead end.

In the year following Daisy's death, investigators questioned over eight hundred people and followed close to 250 leads, all to no avail. The case went cold. All authorities had gathered was that Daisy Zick had been murdered in what was likely a crime of passion, either by a man she was having an affair with, a man who mistook her kindness for romantic interest and then flew into a rage when she rejected him, or the wife of a man she was having an affair with. A criminal profiler suggested that, due to the location of Daisy's stab wounds, the killer had a fetish for large breasts, and that the killer's mother likely had large breasts. The profiler believed that the killer didn't intend to rape Daisy, they just wanted to "look," which was why she was only partially undressed. The profiler believed that in the five years following the murder, there would be other violent activity perpetrated by the killer.

Despite many promising leads over the years, only one man has ever been named as an official person of interest in the case. On January 10, 1967, nearly four years after Daisy's murder, a man by the name of Virgil Pugh contacted police following an incident he witnessed at a Battle Creek bar. Pugh saw a man threaten a woman who refused to dance with him. The man told the woman that he would do to her what he'd done to Daisy Zick. That man was William Newman Daily, the Zicks' mail carrier.

Daily had been questioned the day of the murder, not so much as a suspect, but as a potential witness. He claimed to have seen a man walking down Michigan Avenue around the time of the murder, and gave a description

The Zick home was located on Jono Road in Battle Creek's Wattles Park neighborhood. *Courtesy of Erica Cooper, 2020.*

different from the other witnesses who'd seen Daisy's killer. He'd also told police that when he passed the Zick home on his route that day, a little after 11:00 a.m., the garage door was closed. That contradicted not only other witness statements, but also the known timeline of events. When police called him back in for questioning, forty-two-year-old Daily muddied the waters even further. He insisted that the person he'd seen walking down Michigan Avenue that day was a woman, not a man, and that detectives had heard him wrong.

He also lied about an assault charge that had been filed against him a year earlier. He told officials he'd parked his car four blocks from his wife's dwelling, walked to the house intent on harming her, broken down the door and then assaulted her boyfriend. Police knew this to be completely untrue; he'd been arrested for attacking his former daughter-in-law, who he was obsessed with. These discrepancies, along with Daily's cagey behavior, bumped him right to the top of the suspect list. Detectives also took note of the fact that Daily had a hairstyle similar to the one described by other witnesses. During questioning, Daily told detectives he was preparing to move to Florida, supposedly for work, but he said he'd be back in Michigan soon and would be happy to take a polygraph then. He walked out of the police department that day, quickly left the state, and never returned. And without solid evidence, authorities couldn't make him return for the polygraph. So they had to turn to the people who knew Daily for answers.

They first questioned Susan Denny, the former daughter-in-law involved in the previous assault. She'd been married to William Daily's son James when she was very young, from 1962 to 1966. The couple split largely because of the elder Mr. Daily's behavior. Susan and James were living with William Daily and his wife, Virginia, at the time of Daisy's murder. She recalled that her father-in-law was behaving oddly that day. He told her that he'd seen a man walking down Michigan Avenue around the time of the murder but that he hadn't shared that information with police. This contradicts his later claim that he'd told police it was a woman and they'd just heard him wrong. It's also strange because he did give that information to the police, and there was no reason for him to tell his family he hadn't. Just like there was no reason for him to hide from them that he'd been questioned by police the day of the murder. But he did. He later told Susan, on more than one occasion, that he'd taken multiple polygraph tests in relation to Daisy's death. In reality, police had questioned him as a witness on day one, then completely forgotten about him until the tip they received years later.

These seemingly unnecessary lies weren't the worst thing. William Daily began making inappropriate advances toward his son's young wife and told her that he knew who killed Daisy Zick. But Susan wasn't interested at all. She was so uninterested, in fact, that she divorced her husband to get away from her creepy father-in-law. In the 1966 incident, Daily broke down the door of the home Susan was in with her new husband and their newborn baby, and he began to choke her. During the attack, he called her his wife and insisted that her baby was his child. Police noticed a pattern. William Newman Daily was a man who reacted violently when rejected by women. He tried to strangle his daughter-in-law for not loving him back. He threatened to kill a woman who didn't want to dance with him at a bar. Is it possible that he stabbed a woman on his mail route over twenty times for rejecting his advances?

Police questioned Beverly Iden, a coworker of William Daily's at the U.S. Postal Service. She, too, said that Daily's behavior in the days after the murder was rather odd, and she revealed that he had a dark blue jacket similar to the one described by witnesses. But she said that after the murder, he stopped wearing it. Multiple witnesses claimed that Daily had bragged about how he used to watch Daisy Zick sunbathe topless in her back yard, something the neighborhood boys also enjoyed watching her do. When investigators questioned Daily's ex-wife, Virginia, they became even more convinced that he was their guy. By this point, they had the opinion of that criminal profiler on record, so they asked Virginia about William's mother. She said that the woman was a petite, attractive redhead with a nice figure who was "well-endowed" and that William and his mother never got along.

Is it possible that William Newman Daily, who interacted with Daisy Zick almost every day, given that he was her mailman, had become obsessed with the petite, well-endowed redhead who resembled his mother? Is it possible that he'd mistaken her flirtatious nature for sexual advances, that he'd seen her sunbathing topless and seen other men coming and going from the house when Floyd Zick wasn't home and finally decided to shoot his shot on that frigid February morning? Is it possible that when Daisy rejected him, he flew into a rage, much like he would later do after being rejected by his own daughter-in-law and a random woman at a bar? Were the authorities so focused on Daisy's indiscretions that they overlooked her creepy mailman until it was too late? It's possible. More than one investigator involved with the case went to the grave believing that's exactly what happened. And William Newman Daily, the only official suspect in the Daisy Zick case, took his secrets with him when he died in 2011. All other possible persons of interest in the case have since passed on as well. It's been nearly sixty years since Daisy Zick's murder, so the chances of her killer still being alive dwindle with each passing day. But investigators still hope to close the case.

While it might have been the first, the unsolved murder of Daisy Zick was not the last crime of passion involving Kellogg Company employees.

THE HITMAN

For decades, the Kellogg Company's production facility in Battle Creek offered public tours, during which visitors could watch the magical process of how cereal comes to life and then sample freshly made cereal. Those tours stopped abruptly in 1986. The company claimed it was due to spies from other cereal companies using the tours to steal trade secrets, but it might have had a bit more to do with the three Kellogg employees who had just been arrested for murder, which led to an investigation of criminal activity at the plant.

Sharon Goddard was a forklift operator who worked the night shift at Kellogg's production facility. Born in 1954 to LeRoy and Arlene Despins, she graduated from Gull Lake High School and gave birth to her first child, a daughter, in 1978. In 1981, she met and fell in love with Ricky Goddard of Dowling, the bass guitarist in the popular local band Joshua. Dowling is a village of less than 375 residents about fifteen miles north of Battle Creek.

Ricky Goddard was born on November 12, 1953, to John and Beverly Goddard of Battle Creek. He graduated from Lakeview High School in 1971, where he played baseball and was in band. He went on to attend Kellogg Community College, where he earned an associate's degree in data processing before taking a job with Battle Creek Glass Works, where he worked for fourteen years. He and Sharon got married on June 15, 1984. He adopted Sharon's daughter the following year.

1985 was a big year for the Goddards, who lived in a small mobile home on Gurd Road in Dowling. Aside from adopting Sharon's daughter, officially making the three of them a family, Ricky opened his own business, Wholesale Glass Inc., in Paw Paw. The family also started the process of building a house on their property, and Sharon became pregnant. With so many exciting things on the horizon as they rang in the new year, 1986 was supposed to be full of milestones for the Goddard family. And it was—just not in the way they expected.

In the early morning hours of Saturday, January 25, 1986, thirty-two-year-old Sharon arrived home from her shift at Kellogg to a strange scene. There were erratic, zig-zagging tire tracks in her snow-filled driveway. The storm door was swinging in the wind. All the lights were on, which was very unlike the budget-conscious Ricky. The dog was at the back door, whining to get outside. The Goddards' daughter, then eight years old, had spent the night with her maternal grandparents, a long-standing Friday night tradition, so she wasn't home. But Ricky should have been. The house was eerily quiet. Sharon called out for Ricky but got no answer. And that's when she saw him, face down, eyes wide open, with a gaping hole in the back of his head caused by a shotgun blast. There was no question that he was dead. Blood, brain matter, and hair were on the table, walls, and ceiling.

Sharon ran to the bedroom and called 911, then placed calls to a few family members before going outside to wait for authorities. First on the scene was Barry County Sheriff's Detective Ken DeMott. Blood evidence seemed to suggest that Ricky's body had been moved after he was killed, so suicide was ruled out quickly. Detective DeMott noted that there was no sign of forced entry at the home, so it didn't appear to him like a robbery gone wrong, but he asked Sharon if she'd noticed anything missing. She told him she hadn't been paying attention, which was understandable, considering she'd just seen her husband's brains on the kitchen table. She asked him to look for Ricky's wallet, a jewelry box, a mink coat, her checkbook, and a diamond ring. The wallet and jewelry box were missing, along with Ricky's wedding ring and the gold chain he wore religiously. But the other items were still there, along with other valuables, including a payroll check, a bank bag full of cash, a vase full of cash, and a newer TV and VCR. It became clear to investigators pretty quickly that this wasn't a robbery, but a murder made to look like a robbery. According to Detective DeMott, it was more common for homes out in the country, like the Goddard home, to be burglarized during the day, when no one was around—not in the middle of the night, when most people were at home sleeping. And it wasn't very likely that a burglar would be carrying around a shotgun; they tended to be a bit stealthier than that.

A few weeks after the murder, detectives received a tip through the Silent Observer Program, which allowed citizens to submit anonymous tips about unsolved crimes. A woman by the name of Carol Straubel reported that her former boyfriend had been talking for months about how he'd been hired to kill a man for his boss. She didn't take him seriously, but when she saw an article about the murder of Ricky Goddard in the local newspaper, she knew who was responsible.

On February 18, 1986, Carol's ex-boyfriend Norman Woodmansee, age forty-seven, of Dowling, was arrested for first-degree murder and conspiracy to commit murder along with his boss at the Kellogg Company, twenty-nine-year-old Richard Eckstein of Battle Creek, and Eckstein's girlfriend of the past year and a half, Sharon Goddard.

Richard and Sharon met while working the night shift at Kellogg; she was a forklift operator on the production floor, and he was the supervisor of the machine shop. They began dating in the summer of 1984, right around the time that Sharon and Ricky got married. By the following summer, Sharon and Richard, allegedly, began talking to Norman Woodmansee about killing Ricky. Norman Woodmansee was a man with a past. In 1985, when the murder-for-hire plot was first hatched, he was on parole for selling cocaine to undercover police officers in the Kellogg parking lot. He was also hiding a dark secret that would come out much later. According to Norman, Richard and Sharon offered him $3,000 to kill Sharon's husband. Her reasons for wanting him dead were many; she said he was abusive, secretly gay, and that there was a hefty insurance policy to be collected upon his death. Only one of those three things was actually true. Norman once drove his girlfriend Carol Straubel, the one who would help police break the case, past the Goddard home and told her, "The man I'm going to kill lives there." He was very detailed about the plan. He was going to go to the house in the middle of the night, ask to use the telephone, shoot Ricky, and then take his $600 gold chain and wedding ring to make it look like a robbery. In September 1985, Norman told Carol that the plan was on hold because Sharon wanted to up Ricky's life insurance policy before he died.

Carol didn't take Norman seriously, nor did the several other people he bragged to about the planned hit he was involved in. Norman was an alcoholic and a cocaine addict who was always telling wild tales. He told anyone who would listen about how he'd killed a man in the summer of 1984 and dumped his body in a creek. Nobody believed that one either. During the time that the Goddard hit was "on hold," Carol and Norman broke up. She moved out of his house, checked herself into rehab, and spent the next few months there. It was only after she was released in January 1986 and saw the headlines in local newspapers that she realized just how dangerous Norman really was.

On Thanksgiving Day 1985, the talk around the Goddards' dinner table, where Ricky's parents and siblings had joined him and his new little family, was grim. Sharon was pressing Ricky to up his insurance policy from $50,000 to $100,000. It was smart, she argued, with the new baby coming and them taking on a mortgage to build their dream home. Ricky insisted they couldn't afford it and that it was unnecessary. He already had a $10,000 policy through his company, a $33,000 policy through Sharon's job, and the $50,000 supplemental policy he carried. But Sharon wanted more, just in case. So she asked Ricky's cousin, an insurance agent, to draw up a new policy. Ricky's cousin drove the papers over to the Goddard home on December 4, 1985, and assisted Sharon in convincing Ricky to sign them. Sharon promised to pay for the new policy, which she did; the first payment was made the week before Ricky was killed.

On March 11, 1986, nearly a month after Sharon and her accomplices were arrested, Circuit Court Judge Gary Holman ruled that while there was enough evidence to send Norman Woodmansee to trial, there was not enough evidence to uphold the charges against Sharon and Richard. The strongest evidence prosecutors had was the testimony of Carol Straubel, who said that Norman told her that Richard had told him that Sharon wanted Ricky dead—and that was just one too many degrees of the telephone game for a court of law. So Norman went on trial, and Sharon and Richard went free, although the prosecutor's office immediately filed an appeal on the grounds that the judge had abused his discretion in dropping the charges against the lethal love birds.

The trial of Norman Woodmansee began in June 1986. Aside from the testimony of his ex-girlfriend and two former roommates, who all claimed Norman had told them about the murder-for-hire plot, multiple people claimed to have seen Norman, Richard and Sharon together, even though Norman testified that he didn't really like his boss and only knew Sharon in the context of her being a pretty lady who worked in his building that he would say hello to in passing. The tire tracks found at the Goddard home matched the factory-issue tires on Norman's 1981 sedan—tires that he had replaced the week after the murder. He told the auto repair technician that he needed them changed to shake the police, and then laughed about it. Surely a joke, right?

There was also the small issue of that other murder Norman talked about so freely. Turns out he *had* killed a man and dumped his body in a creek during the summer of 1984. According to Norman, he was driving home from Indiana on July 19, 1984, when he spotted a hitchhiker on I-69, near the Gas City exit just north of Indianapolis. The man was forty-two-year-old drifter and carnival worker Frederick Kuna of Pennsylvania. Frederick was headed to Benton Harbor, Michigan, to look for work. It was a nearly three-hour drive from Gas City to Dowling, where Norman lived, and then another hour and a half from Dowling to Benton Harbor. Frederick was invited to stay the night at Norman's and sleep off the bender he'd been on for days, then finish his trek the following day. By the time the men reached Norman's place, they were both very intoxicated. Norman went inside and got his .25-caliber handgun—not because he was leery of Frederick or intended on shooting him, he testified, but because he always carried a gun on him in his own home, as one does.

Some time passed, and Frederick was still outside, so Norman went to check on him. As Norman approached his truck, Frederick pulled a knife and demanded Norman's keys and cash. Allegedly, he slashed at Norman, slicing his forearm. So Norman fired his gun in self-defense. Frederick was killed instantly when a bullet entered his skull just behind the right ear, severing his brain stem. Norman said he panicked, stuffed the body in his trunk, drove a few miles down M-66, and tossed the body into the creek. He told investigators, "I threw the body over the bridge and went home. I feel bad about it." Investigators didn't buy the self-defense story, though, on account of Frederick Kuna being shot in the back of the head and Norman bragging about the murder after the fact.

Norman Woodmansee's defense in his trial for the contract killing of Ricky Goddard was this: he was a drunk and a drug addict. He liked to tell stories and brag about being a hitman, but there was no truth to any of it. He also had an alibi. His friend and cocaine supplier, thirty-four-year-old George Zugel of Battle Creek, claimed that Norman was with him the night of January 24 and into the morning of January 25. Investigators had placed Ricky Goddard's time of death right around 2:00 a.m. on January 25. According to Zugel, the two men spent the night drinking and partying, and Norman only left the house twice for very brief periods of time, once to run to the party store to buy more beer and once to go to a payphone and place a phone call to a man named Robert Hyslop about rent money. For his testimony, George Zugel would later be charged with conspiracy to commit perjury.

Jury deliberations in the Woodmansee trial took an especially long time. One of the jurors broke her leg in the crush of media and spectators on the courthouse steps the day the trial concluded. She was hospitalized for five days, during which time, deliberations were on hold. On June 27, 1986, right around the time Sharon Goddard gave birth to her second child, a baby boy who would never meet his father, Norman Woodmansee was found guilty of first-degree murder and conspiracy to commit murder. He was sentenced to life in prison. Less than five months later, on November 12, Norman was found guilty for the murder of Fredrick Kuna and given another life sentence. He exhausted his appeals by 1990 and died in prison on January 28, 2011, at the age of sixty-seven, almost twenty-five years to the day after the murder of Ricky Goddard.

But the story was far from over. If Norman Woodmansee was a hired assassin, and a jury determined that he was, then who hired him? The answer appeared pretty obvious, but the American justice system didn't seem to agree. A break in the case was coming, though, albeit from a very unexpected source. George Zugel, Norman's alibi and drug dealer, was not a good liar, as it turns out—or a good criminal. So when a truck driver from South Haven, Michigan, happened upon the sawed-off shotgun that had been used to kill Ricky Goddard over a year-and-a-half after the murder, it was very quickly traced back to Zugel, who had arranged for Norman to borrow the gun from a friend, forty-two-year-old Robert Hyslop of Marshall, the man Norman had called on the night of January 24 about rent, supposedly.

Norman was with George Zugel at his apartment in Battle Creek on the night of January 24, but when they went to a payphone to call Robert Hyslop, it wasn't about rent money, it was to arrange for the men to pick up Hyslop's supposedly untraceable sawed-off shotgun. Norman told Hyslop he needed the gun to collect money owed to him for cocaine. When Hyslop picked the gun back up from Zugel a couple days later and asked why it had been fired, Zugel told him, "Get rid of it. You don't want it." When Hyslop asked him why, Zugel said, "You don't want to know." So the men agreed that if things went south (and they did, quickly) and they were asked about that phone call from Norman to Hyslop the night of the murder, they would say that it was about rent money. Robert Hyslop took the gun and threw it in the Kalamazoo River. When he saw the news about the murder of Ricky Goddard a few days later, he knew what his gun had been used for, so he confronted George Zugel about it, who confessed to him that he'd been promised $2,000 to help procure the murder weapon. In October 1987, Robert Hyslop pled guilty to charges of perjury and took a plea deal, agreeing to cooperate with authorities in their case against George Zugel. That same month, Zugel was arrested and charged with first-degree murder, conspiracy to commit murder, and conspiracy to commit perjury.

His trial for the perjury charge began on March 14, 1988. He was quickly and easily found guilty. His trial for the murder charge was scheduled to begin in April, but in a surprise move, Zugel took a plea deal. He pled guilty to aiding and abetting first-degree murder and conspiracy to commit first-degree murder, and he was sentenced to twenty-five to fifty years in prison. George Zugel died on May 30, 2011, just a few months after the death of his old friend Norman Woodmansee. Unlike Norman, however, George died a free man. He was only sixty years old. In exchange for the plea deal that allowed him to find love, build a life, and watch his grandchildren grow, George Zugel gave investigators what they wanted more than anything: Sharon Goddard and Richard Eckstein.

In a surprise move that no one saw coming—not the families of the victims or the suspects—Sharon and Richard were rearrested on April 9, 1988, over two years after the murder of Ricky Goddard. They were charged with first-degree murder and conspiracy to commit murder. The trial, which was moved to Eaton County due to the level of publicity the case attracted in the Battle Creek area, began on July 13, 1988, and the setup was a bit strange. It was one trial, with two separate juries deciding Sharon's and Richard's fates independent of one another.

The prosecution's case was simple: Sharon and Richard hired Norman Woodmansee to kill Ricky Goddard so that they could collect nearly $150,000 in insurance money and start a life together. Rumor had it that the baby Sharon was pregnant with at the time of Ricky's murder wasn't her husband's at all—it was Richard Eckstein's. The pair denied this, with Richard going so far as to say that he'd had a vasectomy at the age of twenty-four, but multiple witnesses testified that Sharon had confided in them that Richard was the father. One of those witnesses was a fifteen-year-old girl who babysat for the Goddards and even lived with them for a time. Sharon was hoping to take her in as a foster child, but Ricky wasn't having it. This was just one of the many points of contention in their marriage in the months leading up to Ricky's death. Sharon and Richard claimed to have broken up months before the murder, allegedly because Sharon was upset that Richard was seeing other women at the Kellogg factory, but witnesses testified that they were together until at least early January. So, at best, they broke up a few weeks before the murder. When Sharon testified that she had ended her relationship with Richard in November 1985 to "put her family back together," the prosecutor pointed out that not even a month later, Sharon began an affair with another of her coworkers at the Kellogg factory, Dan Leatherman. He asked, "Was the affair with Mr. Leatherman a way to put your family back together?"

Even with a cloud of suspicion hanging over her head, Sharon tried to cash in the insurance policy that was said to be her motive for murder. And when the insurance company denied her claim, she fought it. The insurance company refused to pay the claim so long as Sharon's culpability in Ricky's murder was still in question— turns out, if you kill someone for their insurance money, you are no longer entitled to said insurance money. Also, the insurance company stated that the newly purchased policy was not valid since it was taken out so soon before Ricky's death. The company would only honor the original $50,000 policy. According to the company, "If the policy was taken out in contemplation of murder, then it was illegal from its conception." In June 1986, at the behest of her own attorney, Sharon signed away her claim to the insurance benefits, leaving it all to her children when they came of age.

There were also other things that pointed to Sharon's guilt, things that didn't seem like a big deal on their own, but all together, were hard to discount. This included the neighbor who testified that Sharon had told her she "might have come into the marriage without much, but would be damned if she'd leave it that way," and that Sharon had expressed concern that Ricky, who didn't touch drugs, would "freak out" if he found out she was doing cocaine. There was the male friend of Sharon's who testified that when he ran into her around Christmas, she told him he should come over after February 1 because "the divorce should be done by then," even though neither she nor Ricky had filed for divorce, a process that takes several months in Michigan. One of Sharon's coworkers testified that on the night of the murder, right around 2:00 a.m., the time police believe Ricky was killed, Sharon made a phone call, and was visibly upset and crying.

All of this, along with the testimony of George Zugel and the fact that one of Richard's employees had been convicted of the murder, made for a pretty strong case by the prosecution, one they were confident was a slam dunk. Sex, drugs, rock and roll, affairs, hitmen, insurance money—this case had it all, and the prosecution felt they'd proven that.

The trial of Sharon Goddard and Richard Eckstein came to a conclusion on July 29, 1988. Their separate juries reached separate verdicts within a matter of hours. They were both found not guilty. They were released from custody immediately and were back home with their families before midnight that night, while the men who no one else had cause to hire languished in prison for decades for the murder of Ricky Goddard.

THREE LITTLE BIRDS

When Daisy Zick was murdered in her home in 1963, it sent shockwaves through the Battle Creek community. Things like that didn't happen there, not back then. Two decades later, locals devoured the murder-for-hire trial of Norman Woodmansee like the plotline of a soap opera. But it was the murders of three young girls over a span of six months in the 1980s that truly traumatized Cereal City.

The first was the murder of Maggie Hume in 1982. Maggie was born to Mike and Lorie Hume in Dowagiac, a small city in Southwest Michigan, on April 20, 1962. Three years later, Maggie's only sibling, her brother, John, was born. The Humes were devout Catholics and were very active in the church. When Maggie was in middle school, the tight-knight Hume family moved to Battle Creek, where her father took a job as head football coach and athletic director of a private Catholic high school, St. Philip's—St. Phil's for short.

Maggie was well-known and well-liked at St. Phil's. She was on the cheerleading squad and was a member of the National Honor Society. Her friends described her as fun-loving, outgoing, and stubbornly independent. After high school, Maggie attended Kellogg Community College (KCC), which was named after Will Kellogg, the cereal king. His W.K. Kellogg Foundation donated nearly $2 million to build a new, comprehensive campus for the school in the 1950s. Maggie was in the medical receptionist program at KCC. While there, she met and fell in love with fellow student Virgil "Jay" Carter, a star volleyball player who was one year her junior.

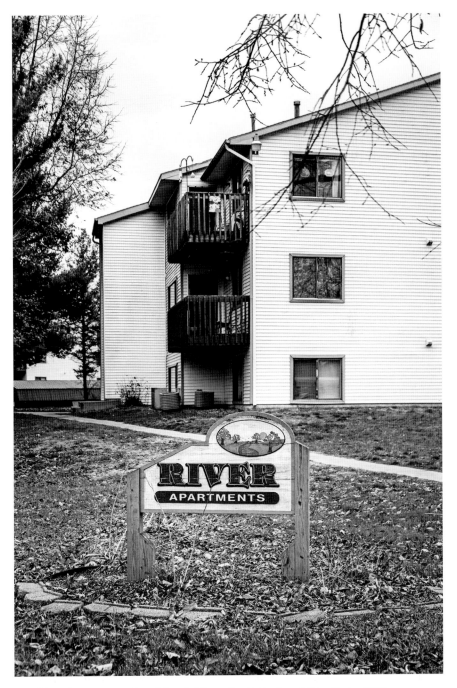

The River Apartments, where Maggie Hume lived. *Courtesy of Erica Cooper, 2020.*

The pair began dating in November 1980, and in April 1982, Jay gave Maggie a promise ring, a thin gold band with a small diamond.

By the summer of 1982, Maggie had moved out on her own and was living at the River Apartments in Battle Creek on the Kalamazoo River. She had a roommate, a girl her age by the name of Margaret Van Winkle, and a good job as a receptionist at a local doctor's office.

And then on August 18, 1982, when she was twenty years old, red-haired, hazel-eyed Maggie vanished into thin air. She was scheduled for the 9:00 a.m. shift at work that day, but she was a no-call, no-show, which was very unlike her. Her roommate, Margaret, had an appointment at the office that morning, so when she arrived, Maggie's coworkers asked about her. Was she sick? Had something happened? Margaret said Maggie wasn't sick and that she wasn't at the apartment that morning when Margaret woke up; she figured she'd already left for work. Maggie often spent the night at her boyfriend Jay's house, so Margaret called him to check in, but he hadn't seen her since their date the night before.

A little after 11:00 a.m., Jay arrived at the Hume home to check on Maggie. She'd only moved out on her own a few months prior, so she often went back home for meals or just to hang out. Maggie's seventeen-year-old brother was the only one there. Jay told him that Maggie was missing, and together, they went to St. Phil's, where Coach Hume was working, getting ready for the upcoming school year. Coach Hume gave the boys the spare set of keys to Maggie's apartment and told them to go check things out.

At this point, no one was overly concerned. While it wasn't like Maggie to miss work without calling, there were a million places she could be. She had a lot of friends, was very social and was taking full advantage of living on her own and making her own rules. That lack of concern changed quickly when Maggie's boyfriend and brother arrived at her apartment building. Her dark-green AMC Hornet was parked outside, locked up tight, with no sign that Maggie had driven it since the night before. When they entered the apartment, they could hear Maggie's alarm clock going off, so they headed to her bedroom. Her glasses were on the nightstand. Maggie wore big, thick glasses—she was essentially blind without them. She couldn't even get up to go to the bathroom at night without putting them on. So the fact that they were in Maggie's room and she wasn't was a huge red flag. Her bed was a mess, the sheets pulled from all four corners and twisted up like there had been some sort of struggle. Maggie's purse was gone, but her car keys were on top of her dresser. Her closet door was open, and the floor of the closet was piled with clothes, which Jay said was not unusual. Maggie's laundry routine was similar to that of many twenty-year-olds—dirty clothes piled up on the closet floor until there was nothing left to wear.

Maggie's brother John went to check the rest of the apartment, while her boyfriend Jay continued to search the bedroom for clues. When John returned, he found Jay knelt down in the closet, rummaging around inside. John asked what he was doing, and Jay said he was looking through Maggie's shoes, trying to determine if any were missing. The boys returned to St. Phil's and told Coach Hume what they'd found. Together, the three of them went to the Battle Creek Police Department to file a missing person's report.

Due to the coach's standing in the community, Maggie's case became an instant priority. There was no twenty-four-, forty-eight- or seventy-two-hour waiting period, or blasé attitude about her disappearance. Police called Maggie's roommate, Margaret, at work and arranged to meet her at the apartment on her lunch break, right around 1:00 p.m. Margaret let Officer Bill Brenner and Detective Nick Pestun in to look around. She said the only thing she noticed out of place was that the closet doors in the main hall were open, and the girls usually kept them closed. The officers did a quick check of the apartment and asked Margaret some questions. As they prepared to leave, Margaret asked them to look around once more, a little more thoroughly. She said, "I don't want to open a closet door or find a body under a bed or behind a couch." So the officers looked behind the couches, under the beds. And then Officer Brenner took a closer look inside Maggie's closet. On top of the pile of dirty laundry was a red-white-and-blue quilt—not wadded up in a heap like it would be if someone had tossed it in there, but spread out, covering the laundry pile. The officer thought that was a bit odd. So he lifted up the corner of the quilt. Under that was a pink-and-white blanket, also spread out. And under that was the body of Maggie Hume.

An autopsy would later reveal that Maggie had been sexually assaulted and bludgeoned, although the cause of death was ligature strangulation—strangulation with an object. The wounds on Maggie's neck indicated that she'd likely been strangled with a belt or something similar. The medical examiner placed her time of death between midnight and 2:00 a.m., roughly twelve hours before she was found. Detectives immediately took in for questioning Maggie's boyfriend, the last person to see her alive, and her roommate, who slept the night away in her bed, just feet from Maggie's dead body.

According to Margaret Van Winkle, she'd last seen Maggie around 6:30 p.m. the night before, on August 17. Maggie was sitting on her bed, reading a magazine when Margaret left for Detroit Metro Airport to pick

The apartment building where Maggie Hume's body was found. *Courtesy of Erica Cooper, 2020.*

up her sister, who was flying in from Europe. Around 10:15 p.m., Margaret called Maggie to tell her that the flight was delayed and that she likely wouldn't be home until about 4:00 a.m., so she told her not to be alarmed if she heard noises at that time. Margaret arrived home around 3:45 a.m. The apartment door was locked—double bolted from the inside—and all the lights were off. She didn't see anything out of the ordinary, so she went to bed and didn't wake up until 8:00 a.m., over an hour after her alarm clock started going off. Already late for work, she ran into Maggie's room, where the nearest phone was, and found it on the floor, off the hook. She called her boss and told her she'd be in as soon as she could, then rushed through her morning routine and out the door, with no clue that Maggie was lying dead in a closet the whole time.

Jay Carter, Maggie's boyfriend, worked the late shift at the Battle Creek Beer Company. Records indicated that he had clocked out at 9:45 p.m. on August 17. After work, he went to Maggie's house. The two had sex in the living room, then ate popcorn while they watched *M*A*S*H* and the evening news before Jay left around 11:30 p.m. or so. During the hour and a half that Jay was there, Maggie got two phone calls. One was from Margaret, who'd called to tell her that she would be home late due to the delayed flight. The other, a short time later, was a bit stranger. Jay claimed that the man on the other end of the phone asked for "my baby, Maggie," and then started talking about the vulgar things he wanted to do to and with Maggie. Upset, she hung up the phone. In reality, it wasn't a prank call at all. It was Maggie's high school boyfriend Jim Downey. He was calling to see if Maggie still wanted him to procure beer for the birthday party she was planning for Margaret. Jim later told police that Maggie answered the phone, realized it was him and then didn't speak, likely because Jay was there. He tried to call her back a few times later that night, but the line was busy.

Maggie and Jim had a strong connection. They'd dated all through high school, during which time Maggie got pregnant and had an abortion. When you go through something that traumatic together, it creates a bond. So, even after they broke up, they remained good friends. There were those who thought it was more than that, though. Even though Jim was engaged and Maggie was promised to Jay, many people thought the two were still carrying on a romantic relationship in secret, including Jay. When detectives asked Jay who might want to hurt Maggie, Jim Downey was at the top of his list. And he was a suspect at first, but officials ruled him out pretty quickly. They were already focused on someone else: Jay Carter.

There were plenty of reasons police thought the boyfriend did it; it wasn't just because that's usually the case. Jay was the last person to see Maggie, and his story about that night didn't add up. He told officials that Maggie had asked him to stay the night. So why didn't he? She was alone, her roommate was gone, and she was freaked out by this obscene phone call Jay said she'd gotten. Why would he leave her there by herself? He said that when he left that night, he heard Maggie lock the door behind him. The deadbolt could only be locked or unlocked from the inside, or from the outside with a key. When Margaret arrived home several hours later, the deadbolt was locked, and none of the keys were missing, so it had to have been locked from the inside, like Jay said, which meant that whoever killed Maggie didn't leave through the front door. They had to have escaped through the sliding door off the second-floor balcony. Jay was known to frequently climb up the balcony when he and Maggie were fighting and she wouldn't let him in. Investigators found shoe prints on the utility box below the balcony and grass clippings from the freshly mowed lawn leading from the sliding glass door directly to Maggie's bedroom. So they were confident that the balcony was the method of entry and exit the killer used. Additionally, Maggie's brother recounted that he found Jay in Maggie's closet that morning, rummaging around. But he didn't see her body? Investigators said that due to the way the body was positioned, that would have been impossible.

While he was being questioned, just hours after being told that his girlfriend had been murdered, Jay was concerned about being late to work, which seemed weird to everyone involved. But things would only get weirder. In the days following Maggie's death, Jay's behavior was erratic at best. He was nervous, fidgety, always coming and going from the Hume home, never staying long. We all process grief differently, so that alone maybe isn't a red flag, but there were other things—like when he asked one of Maggie's friends out on a date before Maggie's funeral. It was also strange that he knew facts about the case that officials hadn't told anyone, even the Hume family—like how the body was positioned and the fact that Maggie had been raped. That information was released with the autopsy report in October, two months after Maggie's murder, but Jay knew. His theory, which he shared with everyone, was that Maggie's death was an accident and that she'd been killed by someone who cared about her, which was evident by the way her killer had lovingly wrapped her body in blankets. He said that whoever killed her must have thought, "If I can't have her, no one can." But the only person who seemed to have that attitude where Maggie was concerned was him.

Jay also failed his polygraph test. When he could tell it wasn't going well, he ripped off the probes and stormed out of the police station. He refused to give hair, blood, fingerprint, or saliva samples. Jay was Maggie's boyfriend, he was in her apartment all the time. They'd had sex just hours before she was killed, he had already admitted to that. So the presence of his fingerprints and DNA at the crime scene wouldn't have proven anything. But his refusal to provide them certainly raised eyebrows.

Several of Maggie's friends told police that her relationship with Jay was not a good one. They fought all the time. Jay was possessive, jealous, and verbally and mentally abusive. Maggie wanted to break up with him, but she was afraid of what he would do. A faculty member at St. Phil's told police that at a high school volleyball game in early 1982, she happened upon Jay and Maggie out in the hall. Jay was choking Maggie, and when the faculty member broke it up, Jay said, "I will choke the life out of her and hide her where no one could find her." There were several witnesses to this incident.

Authorities were pretty confident that Jay was their guy. They were so focused on him, in fact, that they missed some things. On the day of the murder, when they were questioning Jay, they failed to notice that Maggie's downstairs neighbor, Michael Ronning, was loading all of his belongings onto a trailer, getting ready to flee the state. And less than six months later, when another young Battle Creek girl was found murdered, officials failed to make a connection—at least at first.

Patti Rosansky was born on May 14, 1965, in Philadelphia, Pennsylvania. When she was eleven years old, her mother passed away, and she was sent to live with her brother John and his wife. They moved to Battle Creek in 1982, right around the time of Maggie Hume's murder, and Patti was enrolled at Battle Creek Central High School, which is less than five miles from the apartment building Maggie Hume was killed in. Patti was a good student and was taking vocational classes for medical occupational therapy. The Rosanskys, like the Humes, were members of St. Philip's Catholic Church.

On the morning of February 3, 1983, seventeen-year-old Patti was walking to school with friends around 8:00 a.m. Just before they reached the school, with the building in clear view, Patti's friends stopped to smoke, but Patti kept walking. She never made it to class and was not seen alive again.

Two months later, on April 6, Patti's body was found in a ravine near the Kalamazoo River by two men collecting scrap metal in the woods. Her remains were partially clothed and covered with garbage and leaves. The high school junior had been sexually assaulted and bludgeoned to death, her skull crushed. One of the investigators assigned to the Rosansky murder

Battle Creek Central High School, where Patti Rosansky was last seen. *Courtesy of Erica Cooper, 2020.*

was Detective Nick Pestun, who'd been inside the Hume apartment when Maggie's body was found. Before police even had any suspects in the Rosansky case, there was another murder.

Karry Lynn Evans was born February 11, 1966, in Anchorage, Alaska, to Kathy and Larry Evans. Karry Lynn's father was in the Air Force, so the family moved here, there, and everywhere until Karry Lynn's parents divorced and she settled with her mother and siblings in Manchester, Michigan, a little village near Ann Arbor. Like many teens, Karry Lynn struggled and got into trouble. In February 1983, right around the time Patti Rosansky disappeared, seventeen-year-old Karry Lynn moved to Bellevue, a small town about fifteen miles north of Battle Creek, to live with her paternal grandparents. She enrolled at Bellevue High School as a junior, where she played the clarinet in the school band.

March 13, 1983, was a Sunday. Patti Rosansky had been missing for nearly six weeks, and it would be another month before her body was found. Karry Lynn had stayed at a friend's house the night before and was walking home down Main Street when she was last spotted. She never returned home and was not seen alive again.

Two months after she disappeared, on May 10, her decomposing body was found by mushroom hunters at the Kellogg Sportsmen's Club on 14 Mile Road in Battle Creek, just about twelve miles from where Patti Rosansky's body was found. Like Patti, Karry Lynn was found partially clothed and buried under debris. She'd been sexually assaulted and strangled to death.

That's two seventeen-year-old girls plucked from the street in broad daylight, six weeks apart, in the same general area. Both girls were petite with dark hair and dark eyes. And then, of course, there was Maggie Hume, killed just six months before Patti and Karry Lynn. There were some differences between her case and the others, to be sure, but there were also quite a few similarities. And all three girls were connected in a way that officials would not discover for years.

Talk began around Battle Creek of Satanic cults and sacrifices. One of the suspects in the Rosansky case was a self-proclaimed Satanist, and Karry Lynn wrote to friends about Satanic beliefs and wore a red jacket with "666" printed on the back. Also, this was during the height of Satanic panic, so everyone had the Antichrist on the brain. Authorities were overwhelmed. They investigated hundreds of leads, interviewed hundreds of witnesses and potential suspects, but nothing panned out. All three murders remained unsolved.

In the summer of 1984, the Silent Observer Program, which was instrumental in solving the murder of Ricky Goddard, offered a $5,000 reward for information on the murder of Patti Rosanksy. Within days, several people, most of them related or connected in some way, came forward with tips. They pointed the finger at Thomas Cress, a developmentally impaired twenty-eight-year-old divorced father of three who lived just a couple doors down from Patti Rosansky. Prosecutors would later allege that Thomas Cress and Patti were acquaintances, but Cress maintained that he didn't know Patti. Cress was a petty thief who liked to drink and smoke weed. He supported himself by delivering newspapers and doing other odd jobs, like collecting damaged boxes of Kellogg's cereal from the production plant and selling them to his neighbors at a discounted price.

According to Thomas Cress's accusers, who, again, all knew each other, he told them that he had given Patti a ride, smoked a joint with her, and then raped and killed her when she refused to have sex with him. Cress was arrested on July 2, 1984, and charged with open murder. He adamantly denied the charges against him. He passed a polygraph test, but investigators claimed that had more to do with his mental capacity, which was said to be that of an eight-year-old, than the actual truth.

Cress's trial began in March 1985. There was no physical evidence at all—not a single bloodstain, fingerprint, or fiber—that connected Cress to the crime. So this man, with the mental capacity of an eight-year-old, was able to pull off an unplanned, spur-of-the-moment, brutal, messy murder but leave no evidence behind. The only evidence was the statements of those six connected witnesses who were paid $5,000 through the Silent Observer Program for their assistance. On June 5, 1985, twenty-nine-year-old Thomas Cress was sentenced to life in prison for the murder of Patti Rosansky. He maintained his innocence, but his words fell on deaf ears.

So that settled things for officials—kind of. They knew Maggie Hume's boyfriend had killed her; they just had to find the smoking gun. Patti Rosansky's neighbor had killed her and would spend the rest of his life in prison for the crime. Only the murder of Karry Lynn Evans remained unsolved, but citizens could rest easy; there was no Satanic cult or serial killer on the loose in Battle Creek.

However, on September 19, 1986, a letter from the Arkansas State Police was delivered to the Battle Creek Police Department that would turn all three cases upside down. A twenty-nine-year-old man by the name of Michael Ronning had been arrested in Jonesboro, Arkansas, for the murder of a nineteen-year-old girl. He'd confessed and told officials that he'd murdered "lots of girls in lots of states." Since he was from Battle Creek, officials in Arkansas thought the Battle Creek Police Department might want to look into any unsolved cases they had on the books involving murdered girls.

Michael Ronning grew up in Battle Creek and had a very troubled history. He liked to drink, fight, and smoke weed. He had a reputation for torturing animals. He dropped out of high school when he was seventeen and went to prison for burglary and stealing cars. He once attacked a female relative with a hammer. He had been arrested for attempted rape, armed robbery, indecent exposure, and raping a drugged sex worker, among other things. He even married his own cousin.

The first shock for Battle Creek detectives came when they realized that Michael Ronning was Maggie Hume's downstairs neighbor—the one who'd packed up his belongings and fled the state the day Maggie was murdered. He lived in the apartment directly below hers with his wife and paraplegic brother. The next red flag was that after spending time in Texas and California (where two other young, pretty girls were murdered under similar circumstances), Michael Ronning returned to Michigan sometime in late 1982 or early 1983. He was living in the Battle Creek area when Patti Rosansky and Karry Lynn Evans were killed. In fact, he drove down Main Street in Bellevue, where Karry Lynn was last seen, to take his sister to school every day.

Michael Ronning was questioned and confessed in detail to the murders of all three girls. The deal was that, for his confession, he would serve out his multiple life sentences in Michigan, where his family still lived. But there was skepticism behind the scenes. While the Battle Creek Police Department believed they'd stumbled upon a serial killer, solved two unsolved cases, and exonerated Thomas Cress, the prosecutor's office disagreed. They labeled Michael Ronning a false confessor, even though he passed a polygraph test and there was circumstantial evidence that tied him to the murders. To be fair, there were problems with his confessions. They looked to be about 50/50 with facts he got right versus facts he got wrong. Those who believed he was guilty argued that he was a drug addict trying to remember the specifics of crimes that had happened years ago, and that he'd killed so many girls in so many different states that he had some of the details mixed up. Those who believed he was a false confessor argued that the only facts he got right were those contained within the case files, which Ronning and his lawyer were given access to for some reason. Some officials believed he only confessed so that he could serve his time in Michigan, where he would be closer to his family and safe from the death penalty, which Michigan had abolished a century and a half earlier. One problem investigators faced was that all of the evidence in the Rosansky case had been destroyed, including the clump of human hair found in Patti's hand that didn't belong to Thomas Cress. According to the prosecutor's office, this was standard procedure. The case had been closed for years, so there was no reason to keep the evidence. But according to the Battle Creek Police Department, prosecutors were aware of their concerns that Michael Ronning may have committed the crime before they destroyed the evidence. This disagreement caused a rift between the prosecutor's office and the police department that lasted for decades. In the end, Michael Ronning's confessions were ruled inadmissible, and he was sent back to Arkansas to serve his life sentence for the murder he'd already been convicted of there.

But what about Thomas Cress? All along, he'd maintained his innocence and even passed a polygraph. Now, another man had confessed to that murder and passed a polygraph saying he did it. The case against Cress was weak to begin with, and this pushed it over the edge. His attorney appealed his conviction, and many years were spent battling back and forth over whether he should be granted a new trial. During this time, Michael Ronning told the *Los Angeles Times*, "I feel for this guy that's in prison. But I didn't put him there. I have done my best to bring closure to everyone involved in this." In 2010, on her last day in office, Michigan Governor Jennifer Granholm commuted Thomas Cress's life sentence to time served. After spending half his life in prison, he was a free man.

But there are no winners here. If Thomas Cress killed Patti Rosansky, then her killer was given unearned freedom and is now out roaming the streets once again. If he was wrongfully convicted, then he lost twenty-five years of his life so that his drug-addicted neighbors could split a $5,000 reward and the city could quell the public's growing fears about a serial killer on the loose. If Michael Ronning murdered his upstairs neighbor Maggie Hume, well, he's rotting away in an Arkansas prison for murder regardless. But if her boyfriend, Jay Carter, was responsible, then he got away with murder. And what about Karry Lynn Evans? Her murder remains unsolved, with no leads aside from the Ronning confession. Her death seems to have been lost in the pandemonium surrounding the Hume and Rosansky cases. In addition to the girls in Battle Creek, officials believe Michael Ronning may be responsible for as many as twenty to forty murders around the country. Detectives were able to track his movements during the late 1970s and early 1980s, and everywhere he went, similar crimes occurred—pretty, young girls vanished in the middle of the day, only to be found in the woods, in a ravine, or a field somewhere, raped, bludgeoned, strangled, and then hidden under a pile of debris. Michael Ronning maintains that he murdered seven women, including Maggie, Patti and Karry Lynn, but he's only been convicted of one murder out of seven—or twenty, or forty.

THE MONSTER

Probably more than any other time in the city's history, parents in Battle Creek worried about their daughters in 1983—what with missing and murdered local girls dominating the headlines daily. The Golyar family was no exception. Their adopted seven-year-old daughter, Shanna, had already been through so much in her short life, her parents couldn't imagine losing her to a monster. But try as they might—and they did try—they couldn't save their little girl.

Shanna Kay was born in Kalamazoo, Michigan, on June 28, 1975, the first and only daughter of a young, unwed mother and an alcoholic, abusive father. By all accounts, both of Shanna Kay's parents doted on her and treated her like a princess. But there was trouble in the home. In 1967, Shanna Kay's father had been convicted of taking indecent liberties with a child and spent nearly three years behind bars. Soon after his release, he met Shanna Kay's mother, who was a divorcee with two young sons. The home they made together was so unsafe that the boys were removed from their custody and became wards of the state. Shanna Kay actually never met her older half-brothers, but she did have a little brother who was about eighteen months younger than her.

In early 1978, two-and-a-half-year-old Shanna Kay and her brother, who was around a year old, were removed from their parents' care due to violence in the home. Their mother, who was twenty-eight at the time and had already permanently lost custody of her two older children, couldn't lose her babies—not again. So she finally found the courage to leave her abusive boyfriend. As a result, the state agreed to return Shanna Kay and her brother to their mother's care. After all, she wasn't the problem. She was said to be a loving, attentive mother with a big heart. It was just her taste in men that made her unfit.

It was late spring 1978. The kids had already been gone for a couple of months, but they would be coming home within days, and Shanna Kay's mother was beyond excited. One afternoon, with temperatures in the seventies and the sun shining brightly, Shanna Kay's mother walked to the laundromat that was four blocks from her Kalamazoo apartment to wash the children's bedding so they would have fresh, clean blankets when they returned. On the walk back to her apartment, she was hit by a car and killed. With their mother gone and their father unfit in every way possible, Shanna Kay and her brother became wards of the state. The courts deemed their extended family—they had aunts, uncles and grandparents—unfit to raise them. Many of Shanna Kay's uncles had rap sheets a mile long, several of her cousins had been taken from their parents' custody and put into foster care; there was just violence and debauchery across the board in her birth family, and the state wanted to give her and her brother a chance at a good life.

So, just days before Shanna Kay's third birthday, she and her brother were split up and placed in the foster care system. After years of being bounced here, there, and everywhere, Shanna Kay was adopted by Ronald and Theresa Golyar of Battle Creek, and her name was changed from Shanna Kay to Shanna Elizabeth Golyar.

Shanna's adoptive father worked for one of Battle Creek's biggest employers, the Kellogg Company. The salary he earned working for the cereal giant provided a comfortable life for his larger-than-life family. He and his wife fostered and adopted many children over the years. Some of the children were simply passing through on their way to their forever families or during a rough patch at home, while others stayed. Shanna stayed, even though her upbringing wasn't the happiest. The Golyars provided her with the necessities—a safe roof over her head, financial support, an education—but there wasn't a lot of love in the home, as Shanna would later testify. Her parents were strict and devoutly religious, their rules stifling. Still, when the Kellogg Company transferred Ronald Golyar to their plant in Omaha, Nebraska, in the mid-1990s, Shanna went with them. When she turned eighteen, she returned to Michigan, got married at the age of twenty, and settled in the small town of Delton with her new husband. The young couple divorced in 1997.

W.K. Kellogg Institute for Food and Nutrition Research. *Courtesy of Erica Cooper, 2020.*

That same year, Shanna began dating twenty-two-year-old Raymond Nycz, her coworker at Triple S Plastics in Battle Creek. The plastics factory was just a few miles down the road from the cereal factory Shanna's father had worked at during her childhood. Raymond quickly fell head over heels for his new girlfriend, but her insane jealousy of other women drove a wedge between them, and by early 1998, Raymond was looking for a way out of the relationship. His timing, though, was terrible—because Shanna was pregnant. The baby was due in August, and Raymond wanted to do right by his little family, so he bought a trailer for them to live in together. But when she was eight months pregnant, Shanna shocked Raymond and broke his heart by moving in with another man, twenty-one-year-old Glenn Herr. Glenn and Shanna lived in a small house in Emmett Township, the same Battle Creek subdivision that Daisy Zick lived and died in. At first, Shanna insisted that Glenn was just her roommate, but it soon became apparent to Raymond Nycz and everyone else that there was more between them. In her final weeks of pregnancy, Shanna bounced back and forth between Raymond and Glenn, sometimes even staying at a women's shelter when she wasn't getting along with either of them.

Cody Nathaniel Golyar was born on August 25, 1998, in Battle Creek. He was just a little thing—barely six pounds—with thick, dark hair and big brown eyes. After Cody's birth, Shanna's back and forth between men came to an end, and she chose to try to make a life with Glenn. Raymond, Cody's father, only saw his son a handful of times after that. Life was not easy for Shanna and Glenn. Glenn had a son just a few months older than Cody, so there were two infants in the house. Cody was colicky, so he was always crying. Both Glenn and Shanna worked at a convenience store, so money was always tight. They actually worked at the same store, but they worked opposite shifts, so one of them was always working while one of them was always home with the babies. And they were so young—Shanna was just twenty-four, and Glenn was only twenty-one. They both had pretty fresh exes, so there was quite a bit of drama. That would be a lot of pressure for anyone, and it was too much for Shanna and Glenn.

On the morning of January 29, 1999, Shanna got up early with Cody, got him dressed, and then left the house before 9:00 a.m. for a full shift at work. That evening, around 5:00 p.m., she was notified that her five-month-old son had been rushed to the emergency room. When she arrived at the hospital, she was told that Cody's prognosis was grim. Her little baby was hooked up to a ventilator and needed to be transferred to Bronson Methodist Hospital in Kalamazoo, where a trauma team was waiting. But nothing could be done to save Cody Golyar. In the early morning hours of January 30, he died from a severe brain hemorrhage that officials said was caused by shaken baby syndrome. Later that morning, Glenn Herr was arrested and charged with second-degree murder. Baby Cody was buried at Oak Hill Cemetery in Battle Creek, not far from the Kellogg family plot.

Glenn's trial began in December 1999, almost a full year after Cody's murder. His attorney insisted that Glenn hadn't harmed the baby—that the closest he had ever come to shaking him was when he would toss him into the air and catch him, a game he often played with Cody to get him to stop crying. He claimed that the night before Cody's death, on January 28, when Glenn was working and Shanna was home with Cody, she'd called Glenn at work and said, "I dropped Cody. You need to come home right now." By the time Glenn arrived home, Cody was sleeping and seemed okay. The next day, though, Cody's behavior was off; he was abnormally quiet and not his usual fussy self. Glenn's mother noticed Cody's odd behavior when she took the two shopping the morning of January 29, but didn't see any serious warning signs that something might be wrong. When she returned to the house around 5:00 p.m. that evening, she found little Cody unresponsive and called 911.

The grave site of Cody Golyar, Oak Hill Cemetery. *Courtesy of Erica Cooper, 2020.*

On the second day of Glenn's trial, Shanna was called to the stand. She produced several letters that she claimed Glenn had written to her from jail, asking her to cover for him and say she'd dropped Cody, imploring her to lie and say that it was an accident. After this testimony, a recess was called, and when Glenn returned to the courtroom, he pleaded guilty to second-degree murder for the death of his girlfriend's five-month-old son. At the age of twenty-two, he was sentenced to eight and a half to twenty-five years in prison. Immediately following the trial, Shanna moved back to Omaha, where she stayed until tragedy struck again.

In Omaha, Shanna started going by Liz, which was short for her middle name, Elizabeth. She continued to be unlucky in love; she went through a plethora of relationships, but none of them stuck. She had two children, a boy and a girl, who she raised on her own. She became something of a party girl, drinking heavily, going out a lot, hooking up with lots of men, not always clearly ending one relationship before beginning another. Far from her strict religious upbringing in Cereal City, Michigan, Liz was in her prime. She was petite with long brown hair and big brown eyes, her porcelain skin adorned with tattoos. In September 2010, when Liz was thirty-five, she met a man on an online dating site. For the sake of this story, we'll refer to him as Tom. Tom was an IT tech living in Council

Bluffs, Iowa, a city just a few miles east of Omaha. The two had an on-and-off (but mostly on) relationship for several years. Tom was good to Liz; he helped her with money when she needed it and helped out with her kids while she worked. He thought they were exclusive, but unbeknownst to him, Liz was still meeting other men online.

In the summer of 2012, two years into what Tom believed to be a monogamous relationship, Liz met a thirty-five-year-old single father by the name of Dave Kroupa on Plenty of Fish. Dave had just recently moved to the area with his girlfriend of twelve years and the mother of his two children, Amy Flora. Amy was originally from Council Bluffs, so when talk of marriage between the two reached a stalemate—Amy wanted to get married, Dave didn't—she decided to move back home to be closer to family. Dave went with her, leaving behind the only life he'd ever known, but their relationship quickly fell apart after the move. Wanting to stay close to his children, Dave rented an apartment in Omaha, near the auto repair shop where he worked.

Liz Golyar was the first woman Dave met on Plenty of Fish, and he was very up front with her that he was not looking for a commitment. He just wanted someone to talk to and have a good time with—no strings attached. Liz told him she wanted the same thing, which would make sense considering she was in a serious relationship with someone else. But she was lying. Before long, she began pressuring Dave to make a commitment to her, pushing him for more. She became borderline obsessed. Dave, however, had not been lying, and he had no interest in a serious relationship, which he told her over and over and over. They fought—a lot. And their on-and-off casual relationship was mostly off by the night of October 29, 2012, when Liz arrived unannounced at Dave's apartment to get some of her things. He wouldn't let her in because he had a date inside, a woman named Cari Farver. This shouldn't have bothered Liz as much as it did, since she had a serious boyfriend at home, but she was hurt. She caused such a scene that Dave's date left. The tall, beautiful brunette with hazel eyes passed Liz as she exited Dave's apartment, and according to Liz, Cari called her a bitch. The encounter was all of ten seconds long, if that.

Once Dave's date was gone, Liz entered his apartment to gather her belongings, and she and Dave argued. She cried. He asked her to leave. They had a few more encounters over the next couple of weeks, but then they stopped talking altogether. After just a few months of dating, it was over—or so they both thought. But then things started to get weird.

It was mid-November when Liz called Dave, frantic and furious. She wanted to know how Cari Farver, the woman who was in Dave's apartment that night, had gotten her phone number, her email address and her home address. She told Dave that "Crazy Cari" had been sending her vulgar and threatening emails and text messages for days and had broken into her garage, keyed her car, stolen her checkbook, and spray-painted the words "Whore From Dave" on her garage wall. As it turned out, Cari had been angrily stalking Dave as well. He felt awful to have dragged Liz into the whole thing. Who knew that dating multiple women from Plenty of Fish at once could end in trouble? Dave and Liz agreed to meet to talk about everything that was going on.

He told her that he and Cari had dated casually for just a couple of weeks when all of a sudden, she flipped a switch on him and asked him to move in with her. When Dave declined, she freaked out and began stalking and harassing him—calling and hanging up, texting and sending emails upward of fifty and sixty times a day, threatening him, threatening his children. But he had no idea she'd been contacting Liz, and he had no clue how she'd gotten Liz's information. Although, she was a computer programmer with a genius-level IQ. Cyber stalking was probably nothing at all to her.

Dave told Liz that he found out from police that Cari had also ditched her son, quit her job, and dropped off the radar altogether. Her mother had reported her missing just a few days after she started acting strangely toward Dave. On November 21, 2012, police visited Dave at work—at first, interrogating him as if he were a suspect in Cari's disappearance. But after he explained to them everything that had happened and showed them the crazy messages Cari had been sending him, they changed their tune. Cari was bipolar, after all, and had probably gone off her meds. She was likely in the throes of a complete psychotic break. And for some reason, Dave, a guy she'd only casually dated for two weeks, and his ex, who he'd only casually dated for a few months, were her primary targets.

Over the next several weeks, things got worse—much worse. Dave started getting texts from Cari that confirmed she was physically stalking him from outside his apartment. She would comment on what he was wearing, what he was doing and say things to let him know that she was watching him. His apartment was broken into; his belongings were slashed and cut up. Liz continued to get threatening texts and emails as well, and her house was broken into several times. Cari clearly hadn't left town, which was what she'd told her mother, that she'd taken a job in Kansas and was just dropping her entire life, including her son. But the police couldn't find her. Her messages were coming from dozens of devices and from locations all over the country. Police figured that since she was a computer programmer, she was using software to disguise her location.

On January 10, 2013, two months after the "Crazy Cari" nightmare began, Dave arrived home from work and took notice of an SUV in the parking lot that was completely encased in snow, as if it had been there a while. It's not uncommon for a Nebraska snowstorm to bury an entire parking lot, but most people dig their vehicles out within a day or two. This one was still covered, so it stood out from the others. When Dave looked closer, he realized it was Cari's Ford Explorer. He called the police. They impounded the vehicle, processed it, and dusted it for prints, but they found nothing that would help them figure out where Cari was.

The insanity went on for months. Cari was texting and emailing Dave and Liz incessantly, no matter how many times they changed their numbers. The police couldn't find her. Her family couldn't get in touch with her, but she was around—she had to be. She kept breaking into Liz's and Dave's apartments. She was watching them, stalking them. Liz filed dozens of police reports, but nothing was happening. Cari was active on social media. She would send her family birthday wishes, chat with her son here and there, rant about how much she hated Liz. One post even claimed that Dave had proposed to her and she'd said yes. But for all of her online activity and emails and texts, nobody that knew Cari had actually seen her or spoken to her since November 13, 2012, the day she flipped out on Dave.

What was it about Dave? Liz had become completely obsessed with him after just a few months of casually dating, even though she had a real boyfriend at home who treated her well. And now Cari, a brilliant, independent woman, after just two weeks, had gone absolutely insane over the man. If there was a silver lining for Liz in the whole ordeal, it was that the trauma and drama of being stalked brought her and Dave closer together, and they started seeing each other again.

In early August 2013, nine months into the "Crazy Cari" saga, two things happened: Liz and Dave broke up—again—and Liz and her kids moved in with Liz's long-time boyfriend after being evicted from their home. The poor guy still had no idea Liz had been cheating on him for over a year. On August 16, Cari sent Dave an email that said she was going to burn Liz's house down. Dave was so numb to Cari's wild messages by this point that he either didn't see the email because he was no longer reading them, or he just didn't take it seriously—but he should have. By then, Liz and her kids were living with Liz's boyfriend in Council Bluffs, but they were still moving things out of their house in Omaha.

On the morning of August 17, the day after Dave got that threatening email, Liz went to her house in Omaha to get some more of her belongings and found the house ablaze. According to officials, it was a clear case of arson; there were several points of origin for the fires. Liz lost two dogs, a cat and a pet snake in the fire, along with personal and household items. Liz was beside herself. By the age of thirty-eight, she had lost her mother, father and brother—her entire biological family. She'd lost her first baby. She'd lost Dave, who obviously meant a lot to her. She'd lost her sense of security when Cari began stalking her. And then she lost her home and four of her pets. That's a lot. It's too much. But this wasn't just taking a toll on her. Dave was a nervous wreck. He started drinking heavily. He bought a gun. This cute girl he'd met online who said she was only interested in no-strings-attached sex was ruining his life.

Eventually, though, things started to calm down. The messages went from fifty and sixty a day to three or four. Liz focused on her relationship with her boyfriend. Dave moved to Council Bluffs in early 2015 to be closer to his kids and their mom. Amy Flora, Dave's ex, had been harassed by Cari through all of this as well, just not quite to the degree that Liz and Dave had been. But as the years passed, there was still no sign of Cari Farver.

Liz and Dave just couldn't seem to quit one another, and in mid-2015, they started dating again. In October 2015, Liz and her boyfriend broke things off for good, although it would be a few months before she moved out of his house. And then in November 2015, Dave and Liz broke up again—this time, for the last time. But the drama was far from over.

On December 4, 2015, Liz Golyar filed a police report for harassment. This time, though, it wasn't against Cari Farver; it was against Dave's other ex, Amy Flora. She said that Amy had started sending her threatening texts and emails, and she noticed that the tone in them, the typos and misspellings, all reminded her quite a bit of the messages she'd been getting from Cari for the past three years, and it got her thinking. Suddenly, it didn't make sense that Cari, who'd only dated Dave for a couple of weeks, would go so psycho over him. But Amy, who'd broken up with him because he refused to marry her, who'd given him twelve years of her life and two children, only to be rejected because Dave would rather date random women on Plenty of Fish, had cause to behave like a woman scorned. It made more sense for her to be the one to go to drastic lengths to get rid of her romantic rivals. She had more invested and more to lose. Liz told police that the reason she wanted to file a report was because in her latest message, Amy had threatened to shoot her. And Liz knew that in one of the more recent break-ins that had been attributed to Cari, Dave's gun had gone missing. A detective took the report and told Liz he'd follow up with Amy. But before he had a chance, things got worse.

The very next day, on December 5, 2015, a call was placed to 911 from Big Lake Park in Council Bluffs, Iowa. Liz Golyar had been shot and was bleeding out, alone in the dark. An ambulance came, and she was rushed to the hospital, where she underwent hours of surgery before doctors were able to stop the bleeding and stabilize her. She told police that she'd gone to the park alone to think, and that while she was sitting on a bench on the walking trail, Amy Flora had come up behind her, pointed a gun at her and asked, "How do you like fucking Dave?" And then she shot her in the leg.

Police raced to Amy Flora's apartment with guns drawn, only to find her in her pajamas, holding her toddler in her arms. She insisted she'd been home with her kids all day, and a neighbor corroborated her story. She was asked to take a polygraph test. She agreed, and she failed.

Authorities told Liz they were worried she was right—that Amy was the stalker, not Cari. And they said that if Amy would go so far as to shoot Liz, maybe she'd done something terrible to Cari. They asked Liz to help them get a confession out of Amy, and she did. Through email conversations, Amy revealed to Liz that she'd gone to Dave's apartment on the morning of November 13, 2012, and found Cari there alone. The two women argued, then Amy forced Cari into her own vehicle and stabbed her several times, dismembered her body, burned the pieces, put them into trash bags, and threw them into a dumpster. For years, police thought Dave's stalker was Cari Farver, a bipolar genius who fell off the face of the earth after being rejected by a man she met on Plenty of Fish. Now, it looked like it might have been Amy Flora, the mother of Dave's two children, the entire time. It would be another year before the shocking truth would finally come to light.

On December 22, 2016, more than a year after she was shot at Big Lake Park, Liz Golyar, the sad little orphan from Kalamazoo, was arrested for the murder of Cari Farver. Confused? So was everyone else. Here's what actually happened. Liz was completely obsessed with Dave Kroupa and had been from the very early days of their relationship. She was desperately clinging onto the shambles of their non-relationship in October 2012, when Cari Farver entered the picture.

Cari, a thirty-seven-year-old single mother, was a computer programmer at a big-name firm in Omaha, who met Dave when she stopped into the auto repair shop where he worked to have her Ford Explorer worked on. She was gorgeous and very easy breezy—a nice change of pace from the heaviness Dave had been feeling in his relationship with Liz. Sparks flew between the two, but she was a customer, and he was a professional, so he didn't make a move. And then, while perusing Plenty of Fish a few days later, Dave happened across Cari's profile. He sent her a message, and they planned their first date for October 29, 2012, at their local Applebee's. After the date, the two went back to Dave's place. Before they even had time to take their coats off, Liz showed up, unannounced, claiming she needed to get some of her belongings. Dave told her he had a date inside, and she became emotional. So Cari left, and in doing so, she passed by Liz on her way out the door. Despite Liz's accusation that Cari called her a bitch, Dave later told police that the women did not speak. Cari didn't seem upset by the situation at all; she just laughed it off and went home. Liz got her things, she and Dave got into a fight, and then after he got her to leave, he called Cari, who was on her way home to Macedonia, Iowa, a tiny town about thirty miles east of Omaha. She invited him to meet her at her house, and he did. Before they got physical, Cari made her intentions clear—she told Dave that she didn't want a commitment, she just wanted a casual relationship. Dave was more than happy to oblige. That was all he wanted and what he thought he'd signed up for with Liz.

From that night on, Dave was smitten. Cari was beautiful, carefree, and witty, and she really seemed to have her life together. She was a single mom to her fourteen-year-old son, Max, who was the light of her life. Cari was also very close with her mother; they talked almost every day. She did have bipolar disorder, but she'd been on medication that controlled her condition for many years. She'd just landed her dream job and was excited about the future. Cari kept her home life separate from her relationship with Dave, which was easy to do. Her family was in Macedonia, and Dave was in Omaha, almost an hour away.

As Dave and Cari began to spend more time together, Liz became a bad memory, even though she still texted and called Dave all the time. During the second week of November 2012, just a couple of weeks after she and Dave started dating, Cari had a big project come up at work and was working late hours, sometimes until 8:00 or 9:00 p.m. Then she had a nearly hour-long drive home, only to get up at 5:00 a.m. the next morning to do it all over again. So Dave invited her to stay with him for the week, just until her project was finished, so she didn't have to keep making that long drive. Cari asked her mother if Max could stay with her for the week while she stayed with a friend in Omaha to complete her project, and of course, her mother said yes.

Cari said goodbye to her son and mother with every intention of seeing them the following weekend. She went to work on Monday, November 12, and her coworkers had no reason to believe she wouldn't show up the next morning. She slept over at Dave's place that night, and the next morning, he kissed her goodbye and left for work around 6:30 a.m. Cari logged into her Facebook account at 6:39 a.m. and logged off two minutes later. She never arrived at work that morning, and no one ever saw her again. Police believed the account Liz gave them as "Amy" was accurate. She said that she waited for Dave to leave, entered the apartment, fought with Cari, forced her into her own vehicle, and then stabbed her multiple times before disposing of her body by dismembering it, burning it, and tossing it into a dumpster.

By the time Cari's Ford Explorer showed up at Dave's apartment complex two months after she disappeared, there was no sign that a gruesome murder had occurred in it. But then, police didn't process it as a crime scene at first. They were simply looking for evidence of Cari's whereabouts. The only thing they found was a single fingerprint on a mint tin that didn't belong to Cari or anyone else who had cause to be in her vehicle. They ran it through their database, but it turned up no hits. Once the pieces of this twisted puzzle started coming together and they ran the fingerprint again, they found that it belonged to Liz Golyar. And when they reprocessed the SUV as a possible crime scene, they found Cari's blood a few layers deep, beneath the fabric of the passenger seat.

Whatever happened on November 13 happened quickly because Cari was alive at 6:41 a.m. when she signed out of her Facebook account, and she was dead by 9:54 a.m., when Dave received that first off-the-wall text from her, suggesting that they move in together. Dave was shocked by the text and felt like it had come out of nowhere. He told her he wasn't interested, and that was when "Cari" began unleashing her fury on him, Liz, and Amy. In retrospect, it was clear to authorities that none of that came from Cari. It was all Liz. In fact, when Cari's mother, Nancy, was shown transcripts of some of the texts and emails, she was adamant that Cari hadn't written them. Cari was meticulous about spelling, grammar and typos. But these texts were riddled with so many errors that some of them were barely legible. Even if she'd had a psychotic break, was on drugs, or was drinking heavily, there was no way her ability to form a coherent sentence would completely disappear. A momma knows, and her momma knew. But nobody would listen to her.

The same day Dave started receiving strange texts from Cari, her mother started receiving them as well. The first announced that Cari had taken a job in Kansas and was leaving immediately without her son or any of her belongings. It was completely out of character. Cari would never do something so recklessly irresponsible. She loved Max more than anything—she would never desert him. She loved her job and had only been working there a few months. She loved her house, which she'd inherited from her grandparents and put so much time and work into. It simply wasn't possible that she would just up and leave it all. Nancy and "Cari" texted back and forth for a few days, but when Cari refused to return home to explain herself or even speak to her mother on the phone, Nancy knew something was very wrong. The final straw was when Cari missed her brother's wedding, which she had been looking forward to. November 13 was a Tuesday; her brother's wedding was the following weekend. Max was going to be an usher. More importantly, Cari's father, Dennis, was going to be there. Dennis was in the final stages of stomach cancer and didn't have much time left. In fact, the wedding, which was originally set to take place in the summer of 2013, was moved up so that Dennis could attend. "Cari" and Max continued to text following her abrupt departure, and she promised him she would return to Iowa for the wedding. When she didn't show, Nancy called the Pottawattamie County Sheriff's Office and reported her daughter missing. Officers looked at the texts "Cari" had sent Nancy and Max, considered the fact that she was bipolar, and decided she'd likely gone off her meds and left on her own, so there wasn't a lot of urgency in trying to find her.

As the days turned into weeks, Cari's family knew the police were wrong. Even if she had left on her own, she wouldn't stay away. She wouldn't miss so many important milestones—her brother's wedding, just a few days after she disappeared; her own birthday two weeks later; Max's fifteenth birthday ten days after that; and her beloved father's funeral two days after that, on December 12, 2012. Cari had been gone almost exactly a month when the rest of her family gathered to mourn her dad, who'd passed on December 7 without getting to tell Cari goodbye. She wouldn't have missed that, or the opportunity to spend time with him in his final days. And she certainly wouldn't have spent that time obsessing over a man she had met on an online dating website a few weeks earlier. The whole time, though, Cari was still texting from her phone and writing from her Facebook account to friends and family members, which complicated things and confused everyone. In their hearts, they knew it wasn't Cari, but they had to hold onto hope. It was unfathomable that something awful might have happened to her, and it was even harder to believe that someone might have done something to her and was then impersonating her to friends and family.

Cari's parents remained close after their divorce and even often celebrated the holidays together. Shortly after Cari's father's death, her mother, Nancy, had a dream in which he appeared to her and said, "Don't worry, Nancy. She's with me." That was the point at which Nancy began to accept that her daughter was really gone.

Cari's son, Max, graduated from high school in 2016, when police were hot on Liz Golyar's trail, but had not yet made an arrest. For a moment, he allowed himself to hope once again, and he sent her a text that said, "If this is really you, please come back. I want you to be at my graduation." He got no response.

The day Max received his diploma, Liz's arrest was still several months away, but detectives had been putting the case together for over a year. The turning point came, of course, when Liz shot herself in the leg in December 2015. But even before that happened, two determined detectives were onto her.

In April 2015, two-and-a-half years after Cari Farver disappeared, Detective Sergeant Jim Doty and Corporal Ryan Avis of the Pottawattamie County Sheriff's Department asked the powers that be if they could look at the case with fresh eyes. They enlisted digital forensics expert Tony Kava to help. Corporal Avis was going to work the case as if Cari were still alive, and he was going to exhaust every avenue, trying to prove that she was still out there. Sergeant Doty was going to work the case as if Cari were dead and was going to explore every lead to try to prove it. Tony Kava was going to pore over all of the digital data they'd collected—and there was a ton because all of the communications from Cari were made via the internet, so they had tens of thousands of texts, emails and Facebook messages to try to trace. But they also had something else. During the early days of the investigation, both Dave Kroupa and Liz Golyar gave detectives their phones and let them extract the files, which meant the authorities not only had everything Dave and Liz had saved on their phones, but they also had the things they thought they'd deleted.

When they first obtained the files, they were using them to try to locate Cari. They weren't looking to incriminate Liz. But once they reexamined the files with Liz as a suspect, they found a mountain of evidence. Tony Kava discovered emails that were sent from Liz's phone in Cari's name. He found a deleted photograph of Cari's SUV that was taken in December 2012, after Cari and the SUV had gone missing but before the vehicle turned up at Dave's apartment complex. He found a YouTube video posted to a channel that was supposedly Cari's of the front of Dave's apartment building titled "Husband's Cheating Spot." Liz forgot to disguise the IP address on that one, and it was traced back to her computer. Once it was determined that all of the social media accounts, email addresses, and text messages attributed to Cari were being managed by an imposter, Corporal Avis was able to find absolutely nothing that might suggest Cari was actually alive. Sergeant Doty's investigation was much more successful, unfortunately. All signs pointed to the theory that Liz Golyar had murdered Cari Farver, assumed her identity, and then proceeded to stalk herself and Dave for years. One clue was that Liz's filing of police reports—all of the big, scary events, including the break-ins, death threats, the fire—all coincided with times that she and Dave were drifting apart. Then "Crazy Cari" would do something awful, and it would bring them back together. And that fire—the first big, shocking show of aggression from "Cari"—was too convenient. It happened not where Liz was actively living, but at the house she'd just been evicted from, after she'd already moved most of her belongings out and when she and her children weren't there.

After months of detective work, there was already a cloud of suspicion over Liz's head when she showed up at the police station randomly and filed that odd harassment charge against Amy Flora in December 2015. Her real reason for filing the report was that she'd successfully gotten Cari out of the way, but Dave still didn't want to be with her, so she had to eliminate another threat. When she shot herself the very next day, it was all over. Police saw through her desperate act immediately because, as it turned out, she was not a criminal mastermind and didn't know how to stage a crime scene. The only reason she'd gotten away with her ruse for so long was because nothing was being looked at with her in mind as a suspect. But as soon as she came under suspicion, the truth was transparent.

When she shot herself and blamed Amy, the police decided to play along to see if she would hang herself with her own rope. So they asked Liz to see if she could get Amy to confess to Cari's murder because they were tracking Liz's online activity and were easily able to determine that the entire email conversation—both Liz's side and Amy's—was coming from Liz's IP address. This solidified Liz's guilt for detectives, but all of their evidence was circumstantial. There was no body, no weapon, no witness. They only had one shot at bringing charges against her, and they needed more. Time was working against them, though, because the longer Liz was allowed to remain free, the more fixated she became on Amy. Police had Liz under surveillance, so they knew that she was stalking Amy and the kids, who had moved back in with Dave as a safety measure. History was repeating itself, and authorities couldn't allow Amy Flora to meet the same fate as Cari Farver. So, they had to play their hand before they were ready.

Shanna "Liz" Golyar was arrested on December 22, 2016, and her trial was scheduled to begin in May. Prosecutors knew she did it, but they weren't 100 percent confident a judge would agree. Liz had waived her right to a jury trial and asked a judge to decide her fate, which was a smart move on her attorney's part. A jury would be more likely to base their decision on emotion and common sense, whereas a judge was more likely to take issue with the lack of hard evidence—no body, no crime. Just before the trial was about to start, detectives stopped by Dave Kroupa's house to discuss the case. They asked him if there was anything he may have forgotten to mention in all of their previous conversations, anything he might have lying around that had belonged to Liz and could be used as evidence. And suddenly, Dave remembered that he had an old tablet of Liz's packed away in storage. That tablet had a memory card in it, and that memory card had thousands of photographs on it, including ones Liz thought she'd deleted. One photograph in particular was of a decaying human foot that had been severed and partially burned. On the top of the foot was a tattoo, the Chinese symbol for "mother." Detectives called Cari's mom Nancy and asked if Cari had any distinguishing marks or tattoos. Nancy said yes, Cari had a few tattoos, including on the top of her foot—the Chinese symbol for "mother."

Liz Golyar was convicted of first-degree murder and second-degree arson. On August 15, 2017, at the age of forty-two, she was sentenced to life without parole for Cari's murder, plus eighteen to twenty years for burning her own house down. The headlines were sensational. She'd murdered her boyfriend's new girlfriend, stolen her identity, keyed her own car and spray-painted her own garage with the words "Whore From Dave." She sat outside Dave's apartment, night after night, using Cari's phone to send him threatening messages. She burned her own house down, killed her own pets, shot herself, and, worst of all, spent hundreds of hours texting back and forth with Cari's mother and son, posting to Cari's Facebook page and sending emails as Cari. She tormented the family of the woman she'd murdered for years. What kind of monster does that?

Perhaps the same kind of monster that's capable of killing their own child. When Liz was still Shanna and still living in Battle Creek, her infant son was murdered. Her boyfriend Glenn Herr was convicted of the crime, but he always insisted that he never hurt little Cody. He confessed that he sometimes tossed him in the air as a game, but he never shook him hard enough to cause his brain to hemorrhage or his retinas to detach. He maintained that Shanna had called him the night before Cody stopped breathing and said she dropped him. Glenn's defense fell apart when Shanna produced those letters she claimed Glenn had written her from jail—but what was done to verify that those letters were valid? As it turns out, nothing was done. Glenn's handwriting was verified not by a handwriting expert, but by Shanna. Glenn's mother argued that the way the letters were written was beyond what Glenn was capable of. He was mentally disabled and had trouble reading, writing, and comprehending simple concepts. A man like that would make the perfect scapegoat for a woman like Shanna Golyar. Glenn's story about Shanna telling him she'd dropped Cody wasn't something he concocted with his lawyer; it was what he told his mother when Cody was lying lifeless on the living room floor as he sobbed in agony and his mother tried in vain to perform CPR on Cody's little body. She asked him what had happened, if Cody had been injured in any way, and he told her about the phone call he got at work from Shanna the night before. Glenn's mother believed him then, and she believes him now. She warned investigators that Shanna was a master manipulator and a pathological liar. She told them how Shanna claimed she'd had a baby once, before Cody, who died from shaken baby syndrome, but her pleas fell on deaf ears. In 1999, Shanna Golyar was a young, grieving, single mother. The possibility that she was cunning enough to kill her own baby and then confuse a grown man enough to confess to the crime just wasn't feasible. But hindsight is 20/20. Glenn Herr served eight and a half years in prison for the murder of Cody Golyar. Was justice served? Not if he did it and certainly not if he didn't. Liz Golyar is where she belongs now—at the Nebraska Correctional Center for Women, serving a life sentence for the murder of Cari Farver. *Life* is a strange word, though. In the Nebraska prison system, it means Liz will be up for parole review in 2027.

The body of Cari Farver was never located. The closest authorities came was the photograph of her foot that was found on Liz's tablet. It's believed that Liz disposed of Cari's body in garbage bags that were thrown into a dumpster, and that those bags wound up in a landfill somewhere. To honor Cari's memory, the three men who solved the case, Tony Kava, Ryan Avis, and Jim Doty, started a memorial scholarship in her name. "The Cari Farver Memorial Scholarship was established to keep Cari's memory and her legacy of kindness alive by supporting students attending Iowa Western Community College in pursuit of a career in technology."

CONCLUSION

On a warm summer day in Battle Creek, the aroma of freshly baked cereal fills the air. The historic downtown area is in the midst of a massive revitalization project, and the Kellogg name still adorns buildings all around town, from banks to schools to museums. Paved and unpaved roads wind through hills, around forests, and over rivers. It's a vibrant community with a secluded, somewhat sleepy feel to it. Its picturesque scenery and unique architecture make it hard to envision the horrors that have unfolded within the city limits. But then, every town has its secrets—even some that hide in plain sight.

On any given day, thousands of travelers pass by the fourteen-story building located at 74 North Washington Street. Whether headed to work, school, or the grocery store, the Hart-Doyle-Inouye Federal Center barely earns a second glance from most. It's part of the downtown landscape, looming over the city. Home to government office space, it doesn't stand out in any special way from the other buildings in the vicinity, but it is special. It was once the Battle Creek Sanitarium, home to Dr. John Harvey Kellogg's mad inventions and contraptions. It saw the deaths of hundreds, if not thousands, of patients in myriad ways—suicide, arson, murder. After Dr. Kellogg lost the building and the federal government purchased it, it became a World War II hospital that took in casualties from overseas and service members with grave injuries and missing limbs. It would be a challenge to find a structure in Battle Creek that's seen more death and tragedy. It's no wonder rumors abound of hauntings inside the building. Employees

The Battle Creek Sanitarium. *Courtesy of Erica Cooper, 2020.*

have reported seeing shadow people in the halls and hearing disembodied voices and footsteps. It's common to feel an overwhelming sense of dread or sadness upon entering the building, and to experience the sensation of being watched, only to find that there's no one there. Even outside the San, the atmosphere is strange, but the views are breathtaking.

Just down the road from the San is the Historic Adventist Village, a section of authentic and re-created structures of importance to the Seventh-day Adventist Church, including a museum dedicated to the life and work of John Harvey Kellogg. The entire place is teeming with the bad juju left behind by Mother White and her cult-like followers.

On the grounds of the W.K. Kellogg Foundation sits the former home of Will Kellogg himself, a modest mansion that is now used to host special events. While Will lived a mostly peaceful existence, he himself was a tortured soul, never able to escape the feeling of being less than his older brother, despite his world-renowned accomplishments. It is said that his spirit roams the grounds of his former home, searching for the peace he was never able to find in life.

Other remnants of the Kellogg legacy remain, but they are not as easy to find. Dr. Kellogg's massive mansion, known as "The Residence," once home to over forty children, was located at 202 West Manchester Street, across the

W.K. Kellogg House. *Courtesy of Erica Cooper, 2020.*

street from Adventist Village. In its place today is a barren field, without so much as a historical marker. Why was the grand estate torn to the ground? Why wasn't the land repurposed? Did the Kellogg curse make the property uninhabitable?

Where the Haskell Home for Orphans once stood, there is now a residential neighborhood. The residents of the small, single-family homes have long claimed to have issues with things that go bump in the night. Do any of them have a clue why their houses are haunted? For decades, orphans from all over the country lived and died on the property, including the three children killed in the fire that turned the facility to ash. Just down the road, on the grounds of Battle Creek Academy, is what remains of the Haskell Home Cemetery—a memorial stone and marker. The headstones were cleared away long ago, but the bodies were never removed. Ironically, Battle Creek Academy is the flagship educational institution of the Seventh-day Adventist Church, which means children learn to follow Mother White's teachings just feet from where the bodies of children she maybe/possibly/probably had killed are buried.

While the children from the Haskell Home are buried on the grounds of an elementary school, the giants of Battle Creek are gathered just a few miles across town. Oak Hill Cemetery is the final resting place of the

Opposite, top: The estate of Dr. Kellogg, called "The Residence." *Courtesy of the Willard Library Historical Collection.*

Opposite, bottom: The site of "The Residence." *Courtesy of Erica Cooper, 2020.*

Above: The site of the Haskell Home Cemetery. *Courtesy of Erica Cooper, 2020.*

entire Kellogg family. Dr. Kellogg has a modest headstone that's easier to miss than it is to find. His younger brother's plot is nearby, although his memorial is more fit for a cereal king. In life, Charles Post was always trying to one-up the Kelloggs. In death, he finally achieved his goal. His elaborate mausoleum overshadows neighboring memorials in a very literal sense, including that of a civil rights icon. The final resting place of Sojourner Truth is nestled among shrubbery, but that doesn't stop admirers from visiting her frequently. It has become a tradition for those from marginalized communities to leave their "I Voted" stickers on Sojourner's headstone following an election. Mother White and her most loyal followers are buried near Oak Hill's entry gate. Their memorial is visited by thousands of Seventh-day Adventists every year, and it is the reason for the "No Tour Buses Allowed" sign posted on the gate.

For all of the celebrities and historical icons buried at Oak Hill, it is the memorial of an entirely ordinary Battle Creek businessman that is the site of the city's most infamous haunting. When seventy-year-

Oak Hill Cemetery. *Courtesy of Erica Cooper, 2020.*

The mausoleum of C.W. Post. *Courtesy of Erica Cooper, 2020.*

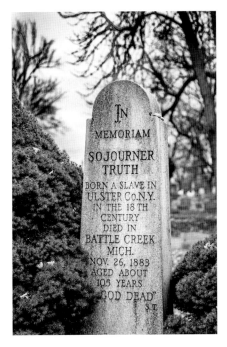

Left: The burial site of Sojourner Truth. *Courtesy of Erica Cooper, 2020.*

Right: The *Crying Mary* statue. *Courtesy of Erica Cooper, 2020.*

old Johannes Decker died of natural causes in 1910, his wife, Ruth, commissioned a Chicago artist to sculpt a bronze statue resembling a Greek goddess as a tribute. The statue stands on Mr. Decker's grave, arms outstretched, a wreath in each hand. This statue has come to be known as *Crying Mary*, and it is said that at the stroke of midnight, every Sunday night, the statue weeps tears. The practical explanation for this is that, over the years, a green patina developed on the statue, as often happens when bronze is exposed to the elements. It just so happens that the patina formed in streaks, making it look like there are tears rolling down the statue's cheeks. But the legend maintains that the statue is that of a woman who murdered her children in a fit of madness and then took her own life. And it is said she cries for her children to this day.

In talking about the Kellogg legacy, it's all too easy to focus on the good—the odd eccentricities, the accidental creation of America's most popular breakfast food. There's no question that the Kelloggs gave more to this world than they took from it. But at what cost? From dangerous medical practices to their war with the Seventh-day Adventists, the

Kelloggs built their empire on the bodies of innocents, and that cannot be overlooked. Those lives had value. While talk of a curse began when the Kellogg brothers were still alive, it gained more traction after they died, when evil began to touch those who worked in their factories and attended their schools. Of course, with tens of thousands of employees over a century and a half, there were bound to be a few bad Apple Jacks. Are the deaths connected to the Kellogg name a coincidence, or is the Kellogg curse something to fear?

BIBLIOGRAPHY

Battle Creek Enquirer. "Girl, 17, Reported Missing for 5 Days; Police Search On." February 8, 1983.

———. "Police Say Girl Died of Blow to the Head." April 12, 1983.

———. "Prosecution Presents Case in Rosansky Murder Trial." March 20, 1985.

———. "Reward Is Offered in Bellevue Murder." April 2, 1984.

———. "Ricky Goddard." January 27, 1986.

———. "Services Pending for Girl, 17, Found Dead in Wooded Area." April 9, 1983.

———. "Services Wednesday for Slaying Victim." May 16, 1983.

———. "Victim Was Pupil at Bellevue." May 16, 1983.

Battle Creek, Michigan. "History." www.battlecreekmi.gov.

Buckley, Nick. "How John Harvey Kellogg Was Wrong on Race." *Battle Creek Enquirer*, March 21, 2019.

———. "3 Children Died When the Haskell Home Orphanage Burned in 1909. Their Grave Is Still Unmarked." *Battle Creek Enquirer*, February 13, 2020.

———. "Why Are There so Many Black Squirrels in Battle Creek?" *Battle Creek Enquirer*, October 14, 2019.

Butler, Mary, and Elizabeth Neumeyer. "A Brief History of Battle Creek." Historical Society of Battle Creek. www.hsbcmi.org.

Cari Farver Memorial Scholarship Fund. "Cari Farver Memorial Scholarship." Pottawattamie County Community Foundation. www.farverscholarship.org.

Christenson, Trace. "Doctor Testifies Infant Was Shaken to Death." *Battle Creek Enquirer*, December 8, 1999.

———. "Emmett Man Pleads Guilty in Tot Death." *Battle Creek Enquirer*, December 9, 1999.

———. "Prison Ordered in Baby's Shaking Death." *Battle Creek Enquirer*, February 4, 2000.

———. "Suspect Shook Infant, Witness Testifies." *Battle Creek Enquirer*, February 12, 1999.

Cohen, Sharon. "A Tale of 2 Men and 1 Murder Confession." *Los Angeles Times*, January 14, 2001.

Collins, Tim. "When Were Cereal Flakes Really Made?" Aired on WBCK on August 9, 2019.

Daugherty, Greg. "Dr. John Kellogg Invented Cereal. Some of His Other Wellness Ideas Were Much Weirder." History. August 7, 2019. www.history.com.

Deane, Ed. "Child Was Tossed, Suspect Says." *Battle Creek Enquirer*, February 2, 1999.

Detroit Free Press. "Contract Killer Gets Second Life Sentence." November 14, 1986.

———. "Orphanage Burns; Three Are Missing." February 5, 1909.

———. "Police Probing Fire Mystery." February 7, 1909.

———. "Two Girls and One Boy Meet Death in Flames." February 6, 1909.

EGW Writings. "Learn About Ellen G. White." www.m.egwwritings.org.

Find A Grave. "Daisy Marie Holmes Zick." 2008. www.findagrave.com.

———. "Ellen Gould Harmon White." 1999. www.findagrave.com.

———. "John Harvey Kellogg." 2000. www.findagrave.com.

———. "Will Keith Kellogg." 2000. www.findagrave.com.

Frances, Franklin. "Woodmansee Admits Shooting, But Testifies It Was In Self-Defense." *Battle Creek Enquirer*, October 21, 1986.

———. "Woodmansee Guilty in Drifter's Death." *Battle Creek Enquirer*, October 22, 1986.

———. "Woodmansee Trial to Open, Jury Seated." *Battle Creek Enquirer*, October 15, 1986.

Fritz, Mark. "Rural Town Fascinated by Sensational Trial." AP News, June 29, 1986.

Gross, Terry. "How the 'Battling Kellogg Brothers' Revolutionized American Breakfast." NPR. July 6, 2018. www.npr.org.

Hardstark, Georgia, and Karen Kilgariff. *My Favorite Murder*. "Live at the Orpheum Theater in Omaha." Aired on Exactly Right in 2019.

Ivkovic, Robert, dir. *Snapped*. "Liz Golyar." Written by Allison Wear. Aired on Oxygen in 2018.

Kellogg, Dr. John Harvey. *Plain Facts for Old and Young*. Burlington, IA: I.F. Segner, 1877.

Lansing State Journal. "Barry Jury Convicts Machinist in Killing." June 28, 1986.

———. "Police Doubt Cult Link in Deaths." June 22, 1983.

Lietzke, Ron. "Body Identified; Murder Suspected." *Battle Creek Enquirer*, April 8, 1983.

Markel, Howard. "How Dr. Kellogg's World-Renowned Health Spa Made Him a Wellness Titan." PBS. August 18, 2017. www.pbs.org.

———. *The Kelloggs: The Battling Brothers of Battle Creek*. New York: Pantheon Books, 2017.

McIlree, Anne. "Attorney: Eckstein, Murderer Not Friends." *Battle Creek Enquirer*, July 26, 1988.

———. "Attorneys Await Goddard Evidence." *Battle Creek Enquirer*, April 12, 1988.

———. "Defendants Testify in Goddard Murder Case." *Battle Creek Enquirer*, July 27, 1988.

———. "Dramatic Trial Draws a Crowd." *Battle Creek Enquirer*, July 26, 1988.

———. "Goddard Case, Round 2: Zugel Trial." *Battle Creek Enquirer*, March 14, 1988.

———. "Goddard, Eckstein Acquitted." *Battle Creek Enquirer*, July 30, 1988.

———. "Goddard, Eckstein Juries to Hear Testimony." *Battle Creek Enquirer*, July 13, 1988.

———. "State's Highest Court Denies Woodmansee's Appeal Bid." *Battle Creek Enquirer*, March 10, 1990.

———. "Witnesses Say Woodmansee Sought Help to Kill Goddard." *Battle Creek Enquirer*, July 21, 1988.

———. "Zugel: Widow Wanted Goddard Killed for Money, Other Reasons." *Battle Creek Enquirer*, April 24, 1988.

Michals, Debra. "Sojourner Truth." Women's History. 2015. www.womenshistory.org.

Michigan's Other Side. "Oak Hill Cemetery and the Legend of Crying Mary." www.michigansotherside.com.

Middleton, Art. "Emmett Twp. Victim Bound and Stabbed." *Battle Creek Enquirer*, January 15, 1963.

MIGenWeb. "Haskell Home Orphanage." www.migenweb.org.

Miller, Bill. "Pair: 'Woodmansee Was With Us.'" *Battle Creek Enquirer*, June 14, 1986.

———. "Wife Tells of Finding Goddard's Body." *Battle Creek Enquirer*, June 11, 1986.

———. "Witness Says Woodmansee Told of Murder Plans." *Battle Creek Enquirer*, June 13, 1986.

Morrison, Keith, narrator. "Scorned." *Dateline*. Aired on NBC in 2017.

Nicolazzi, Anna-Sigga, narrator. *True Conviction*. "The Stalker." Aired on Investigation Discovery in 2019.

NonEGW. "Is Ellen White a False Prophet? Investigate for Yourself." www.nonegw.org.

Pardoe, Blaine L. *Murder in Battle Creek: They Mysterious Death of Daisy Zick*. Charleston, SC: The History Press, 2013.

Pardoe, Blaine L., and Victoria Hester. *The Murder of Maggie Hume: Cold Case in Battle Creek*. Charleston, SC: The History Press, 2014.

Parker, Chuck. "Court to Decide if Widow Will Get Insurance Money." *Battle Creek Enquirer*, September 30, 1986.

———. "Deliberations Resume in Woodmansee Trial." *Battle Creek Enquirer*, June 24, 1986.

———. "Murder Suspicious from Beginning, Police Say." *Battle Creek Enquirer*, February 25, 1986.

———. "Sharon Goddard's Taped Remarks Heard." *Battle Creek Enquirer*, March 6, 1986.

———. "Two Freed in Goddard Murder Case." *Battle Creek Enquirer*, March 12, 1986.

———. "Witnesses: Murder Suspects Had Affair." *Battle Creek Enquirer*, March 4, 1986.

Rule, Leslie. *A Tangled Web: A Cyberstalker, a Deadly Obsession, and the Twisting Path to Justice*. New York: Citadel Press, 2020.

Schwarz, Joe, PhD. "The Enigmatic Dr. Kellogg." McGill. June 13, 2018. www.mcgill.ca.

Smith, Thomas. "Judge Upholds Goddard Ruling, But Says He'd Allow Evidence." *Battle Creek Enquirer*, December 6, 1986.

St. Joseph Gazette. "Wheeler, Noted Dry Chief, Dies." September 6, 1927.

Taylor, Bryan. "Michigan Historical Society Records, Volume 8." USGW Archives. 2000. www.files.usgwarchives.net.

Times Herald (Port Huron.) "No Investigation." February 11, 1909.

White, Ed. "Man Convicted in Girl's 1983 Slaying Will Be Released." *Livingston County Daily Press and Argus*, December 29, 2010.

Wikipedia. "Battle Creek." January 4, 2021. www.en.wikipedia.org.
———. "Battle Creek Sanitarium." December 18, 2020. www.en.wikipedia.org.
———. "Ellen G. White." December 30, 2020. www.en.wikipedia.org.
———. "John Harvey Kellogg." December 22, 2020. www.en.wikipedia.org.
———. "Will Keith Kellogg." December 15, 2020. www.en.wikipedia.org.
Zeman, David. "Evidence of Innocence." *Detroit Free Press*, June 14, 2000.

ABOUT THE AUTHOR

Jenn Carpenter is a best-selling author and award-winning podcast host from Lansing, Michigan. She has been featured on ABC's *20/20* and *Nightline* and by *ABC News*, *USA Today*, and the *Daily Mail*. A true crime buff and lover of the paranormal, Jenn founded Demented Mitten Tours in 2016. Since then, she has crafted and retold countless stories about hauntings and tragedies from her home state. *Haunted Lansing*, her first book through a major publishing company, was released in 2018. Her offbeat podcast *So Dead* debuted in 2019. When she's not regaling the masses with her macabre tales, Jenn enjoys a quiet day at her true crime–themed bookshop followed by a quiet night at home with her house full of boys and dogs. Her interests include researching weird history, collecting antiques, and binge-watching bad TV.

Visit us at
www.historypress.com